# SIGNIFICANT DECISIONS OF THE SUPREME COURT, 1974-75 TERM

# SIGNIFICANT DECISIONS OF THE SUPREME COURT, 1974-75 TERM

Bruce E. Fein

American Enterprise Institute for Public Policy Research
Washington, D.C.

Bruce E. Fein, a graduate of Harvard Law School and a former clerk to a U.S. district judge, is a member of the California Bar and the American Bar Association. He is former assistant director of the Office of Policy and Planning, Department of Justice, and is at present special assistant to the assistant attorney general, Antitrust Division.

348.7346
F32s
99854
2 an. 1977

**Library of Congress Cataloging in Publication Data**

Fein, Bruce E
   Significant decisions of the Supreme Court,
1974-75 term.

   (Legal policy studies ; 1) (AEI studies ; 134)
   Includes index.
   1. United States—Constitutional law—Digests.
I. United States. Supreme Court. II. Title.
III. Series. IV. Series: American Enterprise
Institute for Public Policy Research. AEI studies ; 134.
KF4547.8.F422 1976        348'.73'046        76-55913
ISBN 0-8447-3232-X

*Printed in the United States of America*

# CONTENTS

## 1 OVERVIEW                                                    1

Principal Decisions   1
Issues Undecided   3
Justice William O. Douglas   4
Voting Alignments   4
National Court of Appeals   6
1974–75 Statistics   9

## 2 SUMMARIES OF SIGNIFICANT DECISIONS          13

Criminal Law Procedure   13
Aid to Sectarian Schools and Student Rights   39
Civil Rights and Civil Liberties   47
Elections and Voting Rights   69
Federal Courts and Procedure   77
Sex Discrimination   94
Antitrust   100
Labor Law   111
Regulation of Business   115
Freedom of Information   127
Government Benefits: Welfare and Social Security   132
Miscellaneous: Aliens, Impoundment, Coastal Lands   135

## INDEX OF CASES                                              139

## SUBJECT INDEX                                               143

# 1
# OVERVIEW

## Principal Decisions

In comparison with its 1973–74 term, during which it had much to do with the resignation of President Nixon,[1] the 1974–75 term of the Supreme Court was uneventful. There were at least two factors in the retreat of the Court from politically explosive issues. The first was the illness of Justice Douglas, which was apparently the reason the Court deferred decision on such controversial issues as the constitutionality of the death penalty.[2] Second, the Burger Court has expressed some reluctance to enter the political thicket to decide constitutional questions.[3] During the 1974–75 term, however, at least five decisions that

---

The views expressed herein are solely those of the author and not those of either the Antitrust Division or the Department of Justice.

[1] See United States v. Nixon, 418 U.S. 683 (1974).

[2] See Fowler v. North Carolina, Docket No. 73-7031. Other important cases set for reargument included National League of Cities v. Dunlop, Docket No. 74-878 (raising the issue of the constitutionality of applying the federal Fair Labor Standards Act to employees of states and their political subdivisions); Hampton v. Mow Sun Wong, Docket No. 73-1596 (raising the issue of whether a U.S. Civil Service Commission regulation that excludes resident aliens from employment in the federal competitive service is constitutional); and Alfred Dunhill of London, Inc. v. Cuba, Docket No. 73-1288 (raising complex issues concerning the act of state doctrine).

[3] See, for example, United States v. Richardson, 418 U.S. 166 (1974). There the Court declined to rule on the constitutionality of a provision in the Central Intelligence Agency Act permitting the agency to account for its expenditures "solely on the certificate of the Director." In holding that the plaintiff lacked standing to make the constitutional challenge, the Court observed that the unavailability of a proper plaintiff "gives support to the argument that the subject matter is committed to the surveillance of Congress, and ultimately to the political process." See also Schlesinger v. Reservists Committee to Stop the War, 418 U.S. 208 (1974).

established or suggested the adoption of new doctrine that could substantially affect the future course of litigation were produced.

In criminal law, the Court foreshadowed the possible elimination of the so-called exclusionary rule as a remedy for violations of the Fourth Amendment. It pointed out that the rule serves two purposes: first, to deter police from Fourth Amendment violations, and second, to preserve judicial integrity by refusing to admit evidence obtained by *willful* violations of that amendment. Accordingly, the Court implied that the exclusionary rule should not bar the admissibility of evidence which was obtained by police acting in good faith but which was later judicially determined to have violated the Fourth Amendment.[4] Pending on the docket of the Court for the 1975–76 term is a case that raises the issues of whether the exclusionary rule should apply to the conduct of police acting in good faith and whether violations of the Fourth Amendment should be recognized as a basis for federal habeas corpus relief.[5]

The Court established strict standards of pleading regarding the issue of standing—one of the limitations on federal judicial power to decide cases under Article III of the Constitution. It stated that to acquire standing, a plaintiff must allege an injury which would be cured immediately if the challenged action of the defendant were terminated. This rule may exclude from federal courts plaintiffs whose injuries would not be immediately cured by the cessation of the defendant's challenged conduct because of other contributing causes.[6]

In a decision that may reduce litigation generated by so-called public-interest organizations, the Court ruled that attorneys' fees may not be awarded in cases seeking to enforce rights that significantly advance the public interest, absent congressional authorization.[7] Because attorneys' fees may reach $100,000 or more in complex public-interest litigation (for example, suits under the National Environmental Policy Act), the Court's decision may put certain categories of cases beyond the financial resources of some public-interest groups. Several bills have been introduced in Congress and one has been enacted which authorize an award of attorneys' fees in certain cases involving the enforcement of important statutory rights.[8]

---

[4] United States v. Peltier, 422 U.S. 531 (1975).

[5] See Wolff v. Rice, Docket No. 74-1222.

[6] Warth v. Seldon, 422 U.S. 490 (1975).

[7] Alyeska Pipeline Service Co. v. The Wilderness Society, 421 U.S. 240 (1975).

[8] See, for example, H.R. 7829, 94th Congress, 1st sess. (1975) (authorizing an award of attorneys' fees in suits brought under the National Environmental Policy

Two antitrust decisions of the Court have significant implications. In one, the Court departed from its longstanding rule that regulatory statutes should not be construed as implying antitrust immunity unless that construction is absolutely necessary to the operation of the regulatory scheme. Instead, the Court seemed to adopt a rule of construction that would confer antitrust immunity on a wide range of business activity that is subject to general regulatory supervision.[9]

In rejecting the claim that the "learned professions" are exempt from the antitrust laws, the Court placed in question a host of professional business practices that restrict advertising and price competition.[10]

## Issues Undecided

One of the most notable decisions of the Supreme Court was to set the case of *Fowler* v. *North Carolina* for reargument during the 1975–76 term. That case raises the issue left undecided in *Furman* v. *Georgia*, 408 U.S. 238 (1972):[11] Whether the death penalty constitutes cruel and unusual punishment in violation of the Eighth Amendment. Since the *Furman* decision, thirty-five states have amended their laws to make the death penalty mandatory or otherwise curb the discretion of juries in imposing it for certain crimes. In addition, Congress has enacted the death penalty for the crime of airplane hijacking when it results in a death.[12] Strict guidelines control the imposition of the penalty by either judge or jury under the federal statute. This apparent acceptance of the death penalty by the public may indicate that the Supreme Court will uphold its constitutionality. One important test of whether a penalty violates the Eighth Amendment is whether it is acceptable to contemporary society.[13]

By a 4 to 4 vote lacking precedential value, the Court affirmed a decision of the Court of Claims which held that a government

---

Act); P.L. 94-559, 94th Congress, 2nd sess. (1976) (authorizing an award of attorneys' fees in a variety of civil rights cases).

[9] United States v. National Association of Securities Dealers, 422 U.S. 694 (1975).

[10] Goldfarb v. Virginia State Bar, 421 U.S. 773 (1975).

[11] There the Court held in a 5-4 decision that discretionary imposition of the death sentence as then administered in all states operated so arbitrarily against certain disadvantaged groups as to violate the equal protection clause of the Fourteenth Amendment. The decision of the Court struck down the death sentences of more than 600 persons.

[12] 49 U.S.C. 1472(i), 1473(c) (1964).

[13] See Furman v. Georgia, 408 U.S. 238, 277-278 (1972) (separate opinion of Justice Brennan, concurring).

library could photocopy and distribute copyrighted professional journals without infringing the copyright.[14] Because today the photocopying and distribution of such journals is prevalent, a contrary Supreme Court ruling would have had widespread consequences.

## Justice William O. Douglas

Justice Douglas, seventy-six years old, suffered a stroke in December 1974 which curtailed his work and apparently the work of the entire Court. He filed only 36 opinions this term, little more than half the 65 that he filed in the 1973–74 term. The entire Court produced only 123 signed opinions, whereas the number was 140 last term, and 11 cases were set for reargument, while only 1 was set last term. These statistics indicate that the Court may have deferred decisions in cases in which Douglas's vote might be decisive.

On November 12, 1975, during the 1975–76 term of the Court, Justice Douglas submitted his resignation to President Ford pursuant to 28 U.S.C. 371(b). The letter of resignation made it clear that the pain caused by Douglas's illness was preventing him from performing his judicial duties with the requisite diligence and attention. The stroke that Douglas suffered had partially paralyzed his left side. In October 1973, Justice Douglas gained the distinction of having served on the Court longer than any other justice by surpassing the record set by Justice Stephen J. Field, who served from 1863 to 1897—more than thirty-four years.

President Ford nominated Judge John Paul Stevens of the Seventh Circuit Court of Appeals to replace Justice Douglas. Justice Stevens was confirmed by the Senate by a vote of 98 to 0 on December 17, 1975. He had been appointed to the court of appeals in 1970.

## Voting Alignments

The 1974–75 term revealed clear voting alignments among the justices in the areas of criminal law, antitrust laws, federal courts and procedure, and civil rights and civil liberties. As was noted in connection with its 1973–74 term, the Court seems to be divided into three groups.[15] The votes of Justices Burger, Blackmun, and Rehnquist are generally found to be conservative; Justices Douglas,

---

[14] Williams and Wilkins Co. v. United States, 420 U.S. 376 (1975).

[15] Bruce E. Fein, *Significant Decisions of the Supreme Court, 1973-74 Term* (Washington, D.C.: American Enterprise Institute, 1975).

## Table 1
## BACKGROUND OF SUPREME COURT JUSTICES, 1974–75 TERM

| Justice | Nominating President | Date Seated |
|---|---|---|
| Warren E. Burger, Chief Justice | Richard M. Nixon | June 23, 1969 |
| William O. Douglas | Franklin D. Roosevelt | April 17, 1939 |
| William J. Brennan, Jr. | Dwight D. Eisenhower | October 16, 1956 |
| Potter Stewart | Dwight D. Eisenhower | October 14, 1958 |
| Byron R. White | John F. Kennedy | April 16, 1962 |
| Thurgood Marshall | Lyndon B. Johnson | October 2, 1967 |
| Harry A. Blackmun | Richard M. Nixon | June 9, 1970 |
| Lewis F. Powell, Jr. | Richard M. Nixon | January 7, 1972 |
| William H. Rehnquist | Richard M. Nixon | January 7, 1972 |

Brennan, and Marshall tend to take the liberal view; and the votes of Justices Stewart, White, and Powell are moderate or swing votes.

In criminal law cases, Burger, Blackmun, and Rehnquist voted in favor of the state in all of the ten significant nonunanimous decisions. [16] Brennan, Marshall, Douglas, and Stewart voted in favor of the person accused or imprisoned in at least five of those cases. Powell voted in favor of the accused in three of the cases and White in two. If one reviews the criminal law decisions of past terms, one finds Stewart seeming to move toward the position of the three liberal justices while White seems to have moved toward the position of the three conservative justices and Powell seems to have become a swing voter. In the most significant decision of the Court concerning the exclusionary rule, Powell cast the crucial vote in favor of the prosecution.[17]

In antitrust decisions, a probusiness five-member majority consisting of Burger, Stewart, Blackmun, Powell, and Rehnquist generally voted together in the cases establishing significant antitrust doctrine. Douglas, Brennan, Marshall and White were generally in opposition. The sharp division in the Court over antitrust issues produced at least three dissenting votes in four of the five important antitrust cases.

[16] Eight decisions in criminal cases were unanimous.
[17] United States v. Peltier, 422 U.S. 531 (1975).

Cases relating to federal courts and procedure produced a voting alignment similar to that in criminal law decisions. In the seven nonunanimous decisions, Brennan and Marshall voted in favor of providing a litigant access to federal court in six, and Douglas voted that way in all five cases in which he participated. Burger, Blackmun, Rehnquist, and Powell voted to deny or discourage access to federal courts in all seven. Stewart and White joined the liberal justices once each in this category of cases.

In the six civil rights and civil liberties cases in which more than one dissenting vote was cast, the cleavages in the Court varied. Brennan, Marshall, and Douglas cast votes favorable to civil rights in at least five of those cases. Rehnquist cast votes adverse to the civil rights litigant in all the cases. Rehnquist was joined by Burger in five and by White in four of the decisions. Stewart and Powell joined the liberal justices four times. Blackmun split his six votes equally between the liberal and conservative justices.

## National Court of Appeals

In 1972, Congress established the Commission on Revision of the Federal Court Appellate System. One of its tasks was to study the structure of the federal courts of appeals and to recommend changes that might expedite the disposition of their caseloads in ways consistent with fairness and due process.

In June 1975, the commission issued a final report, which recommended the creation of a National Court of Appeals. The court would consist of seven Article III judges appointed by the President with the advice and consent of the Senate.[18] It would sit only *en banc* and its decisions would constitute precedents binding upon other federal courts, and upon state courts as to federal questions, unless modified or overruled by the Supreme Court.

The National Court of Appeals would have jurisdiction to hear two types of cases. First, it would hear cases referred to it by the Supreme Court. That referral could either obligate the National Court of Appeals to decide the case or give it discretion to deny review. The Supreme Court would retain authority to deny certiorari in any case and thereby terminate the litigation.

Second, the National Court of Appeals would have jurisdiction to hear cases transferred to it from the federal courts of appeals, the

---

[18] That is, judges who are entitled under Article III of the Constitution to tenure during good behavior with no reduction in compensation.

Court of Claims and the Court of Customs and Patent Appeals. Transfer would be appropriate only if an immediate decision by the National Court of Appeals would be in the public interest and

> (1) the case turns on a rule of federal law and federal courts have reached inconsistent conclusions with respect to it; or (2) the case turns on a rule of federal law applicable to a recurring factual situation, and a showing is made that the advantages of a prompt and definitive determination of that rule by the National Court of Appeals outweigh any potential disadvantages of transfer; or (3) the case turns on a rule of federal law which has theretofore been announced by the National Court of Appeals, and there is a substantial question about the proper interpretation or application of that rule in the pending case.
>
> The National Court would be empowered to decline to accept the transfer of any case. Decisions granting or denying transfer, and decisions by the National Court accepting or rejecting cases, would not be reviewable under any circumstances, by extraordinary writ or otherwise.[19]

All decisions on the merits by the National Court of Appeals would be subject to review by the Supreme Court upon petition for certiorari.

The basic reason underlying the proposal was to increase the capacity of the federal judicial system to issue definitive decisions on issues of national law. During the past fifty years, the Supreme Court has heard approximately 150 cases on the merits each term. But the number of cases filed in the Supreme Court has increased dramatically in the past few decades—from approximately 1,200 in 1951 to more than 4,000 in 1974. Thus, the percentage of cases in which the Supreme Court grants review has declined substantially during this period. The Court at present hears fewer than 1 percent of the cases decided by the eleven federal courts of appeals. The consequence has been increased uncertainty in the law because of the failure of the Supreme Court to provide definitive decisions on many issues of national significance. The National Court of Appeals would be expected to decide approximately 150 cases a year, thereby doubling the number of definitive decisions issued each year by the federal judiciary.

Each of the Supreme Court justices commented on the proposal for a National Court of Appeals.[20] Chief Justice Burger stated that

---

[19] Commission on Revision of the Federal Court Appellate System, *Structure and Internal Procedures: Recommendations for Change* (Washington, D.C.: U.S. Government Printing Office, 1975), p. vii.

[20] Ibid., pp. A-221–A-244.

unless significant changes were made in federal jurisdiction to reduce the caseloads of federal courts, the creation of such a court as the National Court of Appeals would become imperative. Burger recommended elimination of three-judge federal district courts,[21] all direct appeals to the Supreme Court,[22] and elimination of the diversity jurisdiction of federal courts.[23]

Justice Douglas stated that a National Court of Appeals was unnecessary. Douglas holds the unorthodox view that the Supreme Court is underworked. In *Warth* v. *Seldon*, 422 U.S. 490 (1975), he wrote: "[N]o Justice of this [Supreme] Court need work more than four days a week to carry his burden. I have found it a comfortable burden carried even in my months of hospitalization."

Justice Brennan also stated that a National Court of Appeals was unnecessary. He recommended eliminating three-judge federal courts and other similar reforms as a more appropriate way to treat the problem of the growing federal caseloads.

Justice Stewart stated that he opposed the creation of such a court at this time but thought it likely that it would be needed at some future time.

Justice White supported the creation of a National Court of Appeals, but without giving it jurisdiction to hear cases transferred to it by the federal courts of appeals, the Court of Claims, and the Court of Customs and Patent Appeals.

Justice Marshall stated that a National Court of Appeals was unnecessary and that reforming federal jurisdictional statutes would be preferable.

Justice Blackmun supported the creation of such a court, to be established initially on a temporary basis. He also suggested eliminating direct appeals of right to the Supreme Court and federal diversity jurisdiction.

Justice Powell supported the creation of a National Court of Appeals and also recommended elimination of three-judge federal district courts and federal diversity jurisdiction.

Justice Rehnquist generally supported the idea of a National Court of Appeals, but had reservations about giving it jurisdiction to

---

[21] There were 267 three-judge federal district courts convened in fiscal year 1975. *1975 Annual Report of the Director, Administrative Office of the United States Courts*, p. XI-72.

[22] See 28 U.S.C. 1253.

[23] See 28 U.S.C. 1332. More than 25 percent of the civil cases filed in federal district courts in fiscal year 1975 were based upon diversity jurisdiction. See *1975 Annual Report of the Director*, p. A-107.

hear cases transferred by the federal courts of appeals, the Court of Claims, and the Court of Customs and Patent Appeals.

Senator Roman Hruska (R-Neb.) introduced a bill, S. 2762, on December 10, 1975, to establish a National Court of Appeals. The Subcommittee on Improvements in Judicial Machinery of the Senate Judiciary Committee held hearings on the proposal on May 19 and 20, 1976. Senator Hruska's bill is based on the recommendations of the Commission on Revision of the Federal Court Appellate System.[24]

The National Court of Appeals, as proposed by the commission, differs in many respects from the recommendation of the seven-member Study Group on the Caseload of the Supreme Court made in December 1972. Appointed by Chief Justice Burger and headed by Professor Paul Freund, that group proposed the establishment by statute of a National Court of Appeals, with a membership of seven judges drawn on a rotating basis from the federal courts of appeals and serving staggered three-year terms. The court would have the twofold function of screening all petitions for certiorari and appeals that are now filed in the Supreme Court and referring those most worthy of review (perhaps 400 or 450 each term) to the Supreme Court and denying Supreme Court review of the rest; and retaining for decision on the merits cases of genuine conflict between circuit courts of appeals (except those of special moment, which would be certified to the Supreme Court). The Supreme Court would determine which of the cases referred to it should be granted review and decided on the merits in the Court. The rest would be denied, or in some instances remanded for decision by the National Court of Appeals.

## 1974–75 Statistics

For the first time in many years, the total number of cases on the docket of the Supreme Court declined from 5,079 last term to 4,620 this term. The number of new cases docketed declined from 4,187 last term to 3,661. The Court heard 175 cases argued, disposed of

---

[24] In accordance with the recommendations of many of the justices, legislation was enacted during the 94th Congress which generally eliminates three-judge courts, except for suits challenging the constitutionality of the apportionment of congressional districts or the apportionment of any statewide legislative body. P.L. 94-381, 94th Congress, 1st sess. (1975).

A bill to abolish diversity of citizenship as a basis of jurisdiction of federal district courts has been introduced in the House of Representatives. See H.R. 13219, 94th Congress, 2nd sess. (1975). There were 30,631 such suits commenced in federal district courts in fiscal year 1975, which was more than 25 percent of all civil cases filed during that period. See note 23 above.

## Table 2

## NUMBER OF PRINTED OPINIONS AND MEMORANDA FILED DURING 1972, 1973, AND 1974 OCTOBER TERMS

| Justices | Opinions of the Court | | | Concurring Opinions | | | Dissenting Opinions | | | Separate Opinions[a] | | | Individual Totals | | |
|---|---|---|---|---|---|---|---|---|---|---|---|---|---|---|---|
| | 1972 | 1973 | 1974 | 1972 | 1973 | 1974 | 1972 | 1973 | 1974 | 1972 | 1973 | 1974 | 1972 | 1973 | 1974 |
| Burger (Chief Justice) | 19 | 14 | 14 | 6 | 0 | 4 | 6 | 4 | 4 | 2 | 1 | 5 | 33 | 19 | 27 |
| Douglas | 16 | 14 | 6 | 4 | 6 | 4 | 41 | 43 | 23 | 12 | 2 | 3 | 73 | 65 | 36 |
| Brennan | 13 | 15 | 15 | 3 | 1 | 1 | 26 | 20 | 16 | 1 | 1 | 2 | 43 | 37 | 34 |
| Stewart | 16 | 17 | 16 | 8 | 6 | 6 | 12 | 7 | 10 | 1 | 4 | 0 | 37 | 34 | 32 |
| White | 17 | 19 | 16 | 4 | 8 | 1 | 12 | 12 | 6 | 2 | 1 | 7 | 35 | 40 | 30 |
| Marshall | 12 | 13 | 11 | 6 | 3 | 3 | 17 | 17 | 7 | 4 | 4 | 2 | 39 | 37 | 23 |
| Blackmun | 14 | 15 | 13 | 9 | 7 | 3 | 3 | 7 | 6 | 5 | 1 | 2 | 31 | 30 | 24 |
| Powell | 17 | 16 | 17 | 5 | 6 | 5 | 6 | 4 | 5 | 3 | 8 | 3 | 31 | 34 | 30 |
| Rehnquist | 16 | 17 | 15 | 1 | 3 | 7 | 17 | 11 | 11 | 1 | 1 | 2 | 35 | 32 | 35 |
| Total | 140 | 140 | 123 | 46 | 40 | 34 | 140 | 125 | 88 | 31 | 23 | 26 | 357 | 328 | 271 |

a Includes opinions concurring in part and dissenting in part.
**Source:** *U.S. Law Week,* vol. 44 (July 29, 1975), p. 3061.

144 by signed opinion, and set 11 cases for reargument. The corresponding figures for the 1973–74 term were 170 cases argued, 161 disposed of by signed opinion, and 1 case set for reargument The Court disposed of 3,847 cases compared with 3,876 disposed of last term. The number and types of opinions filed by the individual justices during the last three terms are given in Table 2.

# 2
# SUMMARIES OF SIGNIFICANT DECISIONS

## Criminal Law Procedure

Since the 1960s, the Supreme Court has typically decided many significant cases involving criminal law each term. The Court did not depart from that trend this term. It wrote full opinions in nineteen important criminal law cases. This trend reflects, in part, the increasingly significant effect that crime has had on both social and political life in the United States.[1]

In contrast, as recently as 1957, Mr. Justice Frankfurter wrote that "review of administrative action, mainly reflecting enforcement of federal regulatory statutes, constitutes the largest category of the [Supreme] Court's work, comprising one-third of the total cases decided on the merits."[2] Today, administrative law decisions of the Supreme Court seldom concern issues of wide public controversy and constitute only a minor part of its workload.

Although the Burger Court has a reputation for favoring the prosecution in criminal law cases, ten of its nineteen significant criminal law decisions this term were favorable to the defendant. The Court ruled that under the Constitution:

—A defendant has the right of self-representation (*Faretta* v. *California*, 422 U.S. 806).

—Defense counsel is entitled to make a closing argument (*Herring* v. *New York*, 422 U.S. 853).

---

[1] A recent Gallup poll revealed that residents of the nation's largest cities named crime as their community's top problem more often (21 percent) than any other problem, including unemployment and the high cost of living. *Washington Post*, July 27, 1975.
[2] Felix Frankfurter, "The Supreme Court in the Mirror of Justices," *University of Pennsylvania Law Review*, vol. 105 (1957), pp. 781-793.

—The prosecution is required to prove beyond a reasonable doubt the absence of provocation to obtain a murder conviction (*Mullaney* v. *Wilbur*, 421 U.S. 684).

—An individual arrested under an information may not be detained absent a speedy judicial determination that there is probable cause to believe he committed a crime (*Gerstein* v. *Pugh*, 420 U.S. 103).

—A lawyer cannot be held in contempt for advising a client to assert his Fifth Amendment privilege against self-incrimination (*Maness* v. *Meyers*, 419 U.S. 449).

—Although preceded by *Miranda* warnings, statements obtained after an illegal arrest are not admissible as evidence (*Brown* v. *Illinois*, 422 U.S. 590).

—The border patrol may not search cars at fixed traffic checkpoints near the border without probable cause (*United States* v. *Ortiz*, 422 U.S. 891).

—The border patrol may not stop a vehicle near the border and question its occupants solely because they appear to be of Mexican descent (*United States* v. *Brignoni-Ponce*, 422 U.S. 873).

—The double jeopardy clause bars prosecution of an individual for the same acts as both a juvenile and as an adult (*Breed* v. *Jones*, 421 U.S. 519).

—The government is barred under the double jeopardy clause from appealing a verdict of acquittal on the ground of alleged legal errors (*United States* v. *Jenkins*, 420 U.S. 358).

The Court also established some criminal law doctrine favorable to the police and prosecutors. In perhaps its most important decision, *United States* v. *Peltier*, 422 U.S. 531, the Court foreshadowed the possible demise of the so-called Fourth Amendment exclusionary rule. Imposed upon the states in *Mapp* v. *Ohio*, 367 U.S. 643 (1961), that rule forbids the admission of evidence obtained in violation of the Fourth Amendment rights of an accused. The rule has been criticized by many because it can operate to permit a guilty person to escape punishment as a remedy for unconstitutional police conduct, even if the police are acting in good faith. As Justice Cardozo described the rule, "the criminal is to go free because the constable has blundered." [3] Others argue that the exclusionary rule is essential to deter Fourth Amendment violations and to preserve judicial integrity by refusing to sanction unconstitutional practices. The Burger Court has indicated

---

[3] People v. Defore, 242 N.Y. 13, 21; 150 N.E. 585, 587 (1926).

14

a sympathy with the former view.[4] The argument that the exclusionary rule is needed to deter police misconduct loses some force because the Court has ruled that federal or state officers who violate the Fourth Amendment can be sued for damages.[5]

At issue in *Peltier* was the retroactivity of the Court's decision in *Almeida-Sanchez* v. *United States*, 413 U.S. 266 (1973).[6] In a narrow 5–4 decision, the Court concluded that *Almeida-Sanchez* should not be retroactively applied. The rationale of the decision was significant: the Court reasoned that the exclusionary rule serves the dual purposes of deterring Fourth Amendment violations and preserving judicial integrity by refusing to sanction *willful* unconstitutional practices. It follows, said the Court, that the purposes of the exclusionary rule are not advanced when it operates to exclude evidence obtained by police acting in good faith and believing in the legality of their conduct. The Court has thus established a constitutional framework for holding that the exclusionary rule is inapplicable to official action taken in good faith.

As it has in recent terms, the Court continued to narrow the application of *Miranda* v. *Arizona*, 384 U.S. 436 (1966).[7] It held in *Oregon* v. *Hass*, 420 U.S. 714, that statements could be used to impeach the suspect's credibility even though they were obtained in violation of the *Miranda* requirement that interrogation of a suspect cease once he asks to speak to a lawyer.

In light of the numerous highly publicized trials of prominent political figures in recent times, the decision of the Court in *Murphy* v. *Florida*, 421 U.S. 794, acquired significance. There the Court ruled that a defendant lacks any constitutional right to a jury totally ignorant of the facts and issues involved in the criminal trial. A person familiar with those facts and issues, the Court reasoned, could nevertheless qualify for jury service if he could render a verdict solely on the basis of the evidence presented in court.

The Court also held in *Serfass* v. *United States*, 420 U.S. 377, that the government could appeal in a narrow category of criminal cases

---

[4] See United States v. Calandra, 414 U.S. 338 (1974).

[5] See Bivens v. Six Unknown Named Agents of Federal Bureau of Narcotics, 403 U.S. 388 (1971); Pierson v. Ray, 386 U.S. 547 (1967). The federal or state official may escape liability if he proves that he acted in good faith and with a reasonable belief that his conduct was lawful. See Pierson v. Ray at 557; Bivens v. Six Unknown Named Agents, on remand, 456 F.2d 1339 (CA2 1972).

[6] There the Court held that warrantless automobile searches conducted near the Mexican border without probable cause violated the Fourth Amendment.

[7] See Michigan v. Tucker, 417 U.S. 433 (1974); Harris v. New York, 401 U.S. 222 (1971).

without offending the double jeopardy clause. Generally speaking, that category is limited to cases in which an indictment is dismissed before trial or in which a guilty verdict is overturned by a judge on a postverdict motion.

The Court decided a case of potentially great importance concerning permissible standards of criminal liability. It held in *United States* v. *Park*, 421 U.S. 658, that a corporate official could be criminally liable under the Food, Drug, and Cosmetic Act for failing to exercise his authority to insure that his subordinates acted to prevent or correct any violations of the act. If Congress should act to extend this theory of criminal liability to several other areas of the law, the conduct of high corporate officials might be significantly altered.

## *Oregon* v. *Hass*, 420 U.S. 714 (1975)

*Facts*: A burglary suspect under custodial arrest was given the warnings prescribed by *Miranda* v. *Arizona*, 384 U.S. 436 (1966). (There the Court held, *inter alia*, that when a suspect held in custody indicates a desire to speak to an attorney, all interrogation of the suspect must cease.) When the suspect requested to telephone his attorney, an officer stated that this could not be done until they reached the police station. In violation of *Miranda*, the officer continued to interrogate the suspect and elicited statements which implicated him in the burglary. At the suspect's trial, he testified contrary to the incriminating statements made to the officer. Solely for the purpose of impeaching the credibility of the defendant, the prosecution introduced the testimony of the officer concerning the incriminating statements of the defendant. The trial court rejected the contention that the statements were inadmissible under *Miranda*.

*Question*: Were the incriminating statements properly admitted into evidence to impeach the suspect's credibility?

*Decision*: Yes. Opinion by Justice Blackmun. Vote: 6–2, Brennan and Marshall dissenting. Douglas did not participate.

*Reasons*: In *Harris* v. *New York*, 401 U.S. 222 (1971), the Court held that statements elicited from a defendant in violation of the *Miranda* requirement that he be advised of his right to appointed counsel could be used to impeach his credibility. The reasoning behind *Harris* was that interrogation abuses were sufficiently deterred by the *Miranda* rule which prohibits the use of the statements for the prosecution's case in chief; and that the protections of *Miranda* should not be perverted into a license for the defendant to commit perjury in his defense, free from the risk of confrontation with prior inconsistent statements. This case is virtually indistinguishable from *Harris.*

> One might concede that when proper *Miranda* warnings have been given, and the officer then continues his interrogation after the suspect asks for an attorney, the officer may be said to have little to lose and perhaps something to gain by way of possibly uncovering impeachment material. . . . [Nevertheless], the balance [between the need for deterrence and the interest of seeking the truth in a criminal case] was struck in Harris, and we are not disposed to change it now. If, in a given case, the officer's conduct amounts to abuse, that case, like those involving coercion or duress, may be taken care of when it arises measured by the traditional standards for evaluating voluntariness and trustworthiness.

## *Brown* v. *Illinois*, 422 U.S. 590 (1975)

*Facts:* Shortly after an illegal arrest, Brown made two statements to the police incriminating himself in a murder. However, those statements were made after Brown had received the warnings required by *Miranda* v. *Arizona*, 384 U.S. 436 (1966). Prior to his trial for murder, Brown moved unsuccessfully to suppress the inculpatory statements on the ground that they were obtained in violation of the Fourth Amendment prohibition against unreasonable seizures. A state court held that despite the illegal arrest, the *Miranda* warnings broke any causal chain between the arrest and the inculpatory statements, thus permitting their introduction as evidence.

*Question:* Are statements otherwise excludable as evidence because the fruits of an illegal arrest rendered admissible solely because they were made after receiving *Miranda* warnings?

*Decision:* No. Opinion by Justice Blackmun. Vote: 9–0.

*Reasons:* In *Wong Sun* v. *United States*, 371 U.S. 471 (1963), the Court held that a statement or other evidence obtained after an unconstitutional arrest or search should be excluded unless it was come upon by "means sufficiently distinguishable [from the illegality] to be purged of the primary taint." The purpose of that exclusionary rule is to protect Fourth Amendment guarantees in two respects: by deterring lawless official conduct and by preserving judicial integrity through refusal to sanction the use of illegally obtained evidence. *Miranda* warnings, in contrast, are not designed to serve these Fourth Amendment values. They are primarily a procedural safeguard to protect Fifth Amendment rights against compulsory self-incrimination.

> If *Miranda* warnings, by themselves, were held to attenuate the taint of an unconstitutional arrest, regardless of how wanton and purposeful the Fourth Amendment violation, the effect of the exclusionary rule would be substantially diluted. . . . Arrests made without warrant or without probable cause, for questioning or "investigation," would be encouraged by the knowledge that evidence derived therefrom hopefully could be made admissible at trial by the simple expedient of giving *Miranda* warnings. Any incentive to avoid Fourth Amendment violations would be eviscerated by making the warnings, in effect, a "cure-all," and the constitutional guarantee against unlawful searches and seizures could be said to be reduced to "a form of words."

Accordingly, *Miranda* warnings per se do not make an act sufficiently a product of free will to break, for Fourth Amendment purposes, a causal connection between an illegal arrest and a confession. In this case, "Brown's first statement was separated from his illegal arrest by less than two hours, and there was no intervening event of significance whatsoever." His second statement was clearly the fruit of the first. In addition, the illegality of the arrest was obvious and virtually conceded by the arresting officers. In these circumstances, the two statements were clearly not purged of the initial illegality and should have been suppressed.

## *Maness* v. *Meyers*, 419 U.S. 449 (1975)

*Facts:* In a state civil suit to enjoin the alleged illegal distribution of obscene matter, a lawyer advised his client that he could refuse to produce magazines demanded by a *subpoena duces tecum* on the ground that they were protected by the Fifth Amendment privilege against self-incrimination. Although the trial judge rejected that claim and ordered the subpoenaed magazines produced, the client refused to comply with the order in reliance on the advice of his lawyer. Consequently, the judge held the lawyer in contempt of court for advising his client that he had the right under the Fifth Amendment to refuse to produce the magazines notwithstanding the court order to the contrary.

*Question:* May a lawyer be held in contempt for advising his client, during the trial of a civil case, to refuse to produce material demanded by a subpoena, when the lawyer believes in good faith that the material may tend to incriminate his client?

*Decision:* No. Opinion by Chief Justice Burger. Vote 9–0.

*Reasons:* As a general rule "all orders and judgments of courts must be complied with promptly. If a person to whom a court directs an order believes that order is incorrect the remedy is to appeal, but absent a stay, to comply promptly with the order pending appeal." In some cases, however, compliance with a court order could cause irreparable injury which an appellate vindication could not totally repair. In these situations a party may refuse compliance and risk an adjudication of contempt in order to obtain immediate appellate review. "This method of achieving precompliance review is particularly appropriate where the Fifth Amendment privilege against self-incrimination is involved." For a party to comply with an order requiring production of evidence protected by the Fifth Amendment would be to surrender the very protection which the privilege against self-incrimination is designed to guarantee.

> Thus in advising his client to resist and risk a contempt citation, thereby allowing precompliance appellate review of the claim, [the lawyer] counseled a familiar procedure. . . .
> The privilege against compelled self-incrimination would be drained of its meaning if counsel, being lawfully present, as here, could be penalized for advising his client in good faith to assert it. The assertion of a testimonial privilege, as of many other rights, often depends upon legal advice from someone who is trained and skilled in the subject matter, and who may offer a more objective opinion. A layman may not be aware of the precise scope, the nuances, and boundaries of his Fifth Amendment privilege.

If a lawyer could be punished for advising a client to claim his Fifth Amendment privilege, then

> there is a genuine risk that a witness exposed to possible self-incrimination will not be advised of his right. Then the witness may be deprived of the opportunity to decide whether or not to assert the privilege. . . . When a witness is . . . advised [to assert his privilege against self-incrimination] the advice becomes an integral part of the protection accorded the witness by the Fifth Amendment.

## *United States* v. *Wilson*, 420 U.S. 332 (1975)

*Facts:* After the jury found the defendant guilty of a federal offense, the district court dismissed the indictment on a postverdict motion. It ruled that the delay between the offense and indictment had prejudiced the defendant and that dismissal was justified under *United States* v. *Marion*, 404 U.S. 307 (1971). (There the Court concluded that if preindictment delays substantially prejudiced a defendant—for example, through loss of alibi witnesses, destruction of material evidence, or impairment of memories—and if the delay was intended to gain a tactical advantage over the defendant at trial, then the due process clause of the Fifth Amendment would require dismissal of the indictment.) The government sought to appeal the dismissal pursuant to 18 U.S.C. 3731. The court of appeals dismissed the appeal on the ground that under the double jeopardy clause of the Fifth Amendment, the government could not appeal the acquittal, even though it was rendered by a judge after the jury had returned a verdict of guilty.

*Question:* Did the double jeopardy clause of the Fifth Amendment bar the government's appeal?

*Decision:* No. Opinion by Justice Marshall. Vote: 7-2, Douglas and Brennan dissenting.

*Reasons:* The legislative history of the Criminal Appeals Act passed in 1970 makes clear that it was intended to authorize government appeals in criminal cases whenever they are permitted by the Constitution. The district court's order dismissing the indictment was thus appealable unless barred by the double jeopardy clause.

The constitutional history of that clause "suggests that it was directed at the threat of multiple prosecutions, not at Government appeals, at least where those appeals would not require a new trial." Past decisions construing the double jeopardy clause support this view. In *North Carolina* v. *Pearce*, 395 U.S. 711 (1969), the Court noted that the clause provides three related protections: "It protects against a second prosecution for the same offense after acquittal. It protects against a second prosecution for the same offense after conviction. And it protects against multiple punishments for the same offense." These protections have similar purposes.

> When a defendant has been once convicted and punished for a particular crime, principles of fairness and finality require that he not be subjected to the possibility of further punish-

ment by being again tried or sentenced for the same offense. . . . When a defendant has been acquitted of an offense, the Clause guarantees that the State shall not be permitted to make repeated attempts to convict him, "thereby subjecting him to embarrassment, expense and ordeal and compelling him to live in a continuing state of anxiety and insecurity, as well as enhancing the possibility that even though innocent he may be found guilty."

None of these purposes would be offended, however, if the government is permitted to appeal in cases in which a "judge rules in favor of the defendant after a verdict of guilty has been entered by the trier of fact." Reversal on appeal would merely reinstate the verdict.

## United States v. Jenkins, 420 U.S. 358 (1975)

*Facts:* After Jenkins was ordered to report for induction, he applied to his local draft board for a conscientious objector (CO) classification. The board refused to postpone induction pending determination of the CO claim, and Jenkins was subsequently indicted for failing to report for induction. After trial in the federal district court, written findings of fact and conclusions of law were filed by the court, and the indictment was dismissed. The court acknowledged that Jenkins had failed to report for induction as ordered and that under *Ehlert* v. *United States*, 402 U.S. 99 (1971), a local draft board is not required to entertain CO claims arising between notice of induction and the scheduled induction date. The court reasoned, however, that since *Ehlert* had not been decided when Jenkins failed to report and since at that time the governing law of the circuit entitled him to a postponement of induction until the board considered his CO claim, it would be unfair to apply *Ehlert* in his case.

The government sought to appeal the dismissal on the ground that the district court had erroneously failed to apply *Ehlert* retroactively. The court of appeals ruled that the appeal was barred by the double jeopardy clause of the Fifth Amendment.

*Question:* Was the government's appeal barred by the double jeopardy clause?

*Decision:* Yes. Opinion by Justice Rehnquist. Vote: 9–0.

*Reasons:* United States v. *Wilson*, 421 U.S. 309 (1975), concluded that the double jeopardy clause "does not prohibit an appeal by the Government providing that a retrial would not be required in the event the Government is successful in its appeal." In this case, it is unclear whether the district court found the defendant guilty of the offense charged.

> The court's opinion certainly contains no general finding of guilt, and although the specific findings resolved against [Jenkins] many of the component elements of the offense, there is no finding on the statutory element of "knowledge." . . . [S]uch an omission may have reflected [the judge's] conclusion that the Government had failed to establish the requisite criminal intent beyond a reasonable doubt.

Accordingly, if the appeal by the government had been successful, there could have been no reinstatement of a verdict of guilty.

> [F]urther proceedings of some sort, devoted to the resolution of factual issues going to the elements of the offense charged, would have been required upon reversal and remand. Even if the District Court were to receive no additional evidence, it would still be necessary for it to make supplemental findings.

Accordingly, *Wilson* does not govern this case.

The government contended, nevertheless, that the double jeopardy clause should be construed to permit appeals, at least in bench trials, which if successful might result in reopening a case for the admission of additional evidence or remanding for more explicit findings by the district court. That construction, however, would undermine a principal purpose of the clause: to prevent the state, with all its resources and power, to make repeated attempts to convict a person for an alleged offense.

## *Serfass* v. *United States,* 420 U.S. 377 (1975)

*Facts:* After receiving an induction order, Serfass filed a claim for conscientious objector (CO) status with his local draft board. The board refused to consider his claim and informed him of his obligation to report for induction. Subsequently, Serfass was indicted for willfully failing to report for induction. Serfass's pretrial motion to dismiss the indictment on the ground that the local board gave inadequate reasons for refusing to consider his claim to CO status was granted. The United States appealed the dismissal under 18 U.S.C. 3731 (1964). Serfass contended that the court of appeals lacked jurisdiction to hear the appeal because further prosecution was prohibited by the double jeopardy clause of the Fifth Amendment.

*Question:* Was the government's appeal barred by the double jeopardy clause?

*Decision:* No. Opinion by Chief Justice Burger. Vote: 8–1, Douglas dissenting.

*Reasons:* Quoting from *Green* v. *United States,* 355 U.S. 184 (1957), the Court stated that

> the constitutional prohibition against "double jeopardy" was designed to protect an individual from being subjected to the hazards of trial and possible conviction more than once for an alleged offense. . . . The underlying idea, one that is deeply ingrained in at least the Anglo-American system of jurisprudence, is that the state, with all its resources and power, should not be allowed to make repeated attempts to convict a person for an alleged offense, thereby subjecting him to embarrassment, expense and ordeal and compelling him to live in a state of anxiety and insecurity, as well as enhancing the possibility that even though innocent he may be found guilty.

In light of the purposes of the clause, the Court has concluded that "jeopardy does not attach, and the constitutional prohibition can have no application until a defendant is 'put to trial before the trier of facts, whether the trier be a jury or judge.' " The reasons for this rule are that "[w]hen a criminal prosecution is terminated prior to trial, an accused is often spared much of the expense, delay, strain, and embarrassment which attend a trial," and in such circumstances an appeal would not permit the "prosecutor to seek to persuade a second trier of fact of the defendant's guilt after having failed with the first." In this case, jeopardy had not attached when the indictment was dismissed because Serfass was not then, nor has he ever been "put to trial before the trier of facts." Accordingly, the appeal was not barred by the double jeopardy clause.

## *Breed* v. *Jones,* 421 U.S. 519 (1975)

*Facts:* A California juvenile court found that Jones, a minor, had committed acts which would have constituted robbery if committed by an adult. After hearings at which testimony was taken as authorized by California law, the juvenile court found Jones unfit for treatment as a juvenile and ordered that he be prosecuted as an adult. After trial and conviction of robbery, Jones sought habeas corpus relief on the ground that his prosecution as an adult violated the double jeopardy clause of the Fifth Amendment.

*Question:* Does the double jeopardy clause bar prosecution of an individual as an adult for the same acts which resulted in a finding by a juvenile court that the individual had violated a criminal statute?

*Decision:* Yes. Opinion by Chief Justice Burger. Vote: 9–0.

*Reasons:* The double jeopardy clause bars a state from attempting to prosecute an individual twice for the same offense. A proceeding which is not essentially criminal is not a prosecution for purposes of the clause. The claim that juvenile court proceedings are not essentially criminal, however, cannot be accepted.

> Although the juvenile court system had its genesis in the desire to provide a distinctive procedure and setting to deal with the problems of youth, including those manifested by antisocial conduct, our decisions in recent years have recognized that there is a gap between the originally benign conception of the system and its realities. . . . [T]he Court's response to that perception has been to make applicable in juvenile proceedings constitutional guarantees associated with traditional criminal prosecutions [except for the right to jury trial]. . . . [I]t is simply too late in the day to conclude . . . that a juvenile is not put in jeopardy at a proceeding whose object is to determine whether he has committed acts that violate a criminal law and whose potential consequences include both the stigma inherent in such a determination and the deprivation of liberty for many years.

Accordingly, the juvenile court proceedings placed Jones in jeopardy for the same offense for which he was convicted as an adult.

It is argued, nevertheless, that no new jeopardy attached at Jones's trial as an adult because it was merely a continuation of the juvenile proceedings. The double jeopardy clause protects against the potential risk of punishment, however, and that potential existed in both proceedings.

The Court noted that its holding

> require[d] only that, whatever the relevant criteria, and whatever the evidence demanded, a State determine whether it wants to treat a juvenile within the juvenile court system before entering upon a proceeding that may result in an adjudication that he has violated a criminal law and in a substantial deprivation of liberty, rather than subject him to the expense, delay, strain and embarrassment of two such proceedings.

## *Faretta* v. *California,* 422 U.S. 806 (1975)

*Facts:* A state court refused to permit a criminal defendant to represent himself at trial without the assistance of counsel. A public defender was appointed as defense counsel despite the defendant's objection. The defendant sought review of his conviction on the ground that the Sixth Amendment guaranteed a right of self-representation.

*Question:* Does a defendant in a state criminal trial have a Sixth Amendment right to proceed without counsel when he voluntarily and intelligently elects to do so?

*Decision:* Yes. Opinion by Justice Stewart. Vote: 6–3, Burger, Blackmun, and Rehnquist dissenting.

*Reasons:* The Court reasoned that "the right of self-representation finds support in the structure of the Sixth Amendment, as well as in English and colonial jurisprudence from which the Amendment emerged." The Sixth Amendment grants to the accused, personally, several rights, including a right "to have the Assistance of Counsel for his defense."

> The language and spirit of the Sixth Amendment contemplate that counsel, like the other defense tools [it guarantees], shall be an aid to a willing defendant—not an organ of the State interposed between an unwilling defendant and his right to defend himself personally. To thrust counsel upon the accused, against his considered wish, thus violates the logic of the Amendment.

The Court noted, however, that

> when an accused manages his own defense, he relinquishes, as a purely factual matter, many of the traditional benefits associated with the right to counsel. For this reason, in order to represent himself, the accused must "knowingly and intelligently" forego those relinquished benefits. . . . Although a defendant need not himself have the skill and experience of a lawyer in order competently and intelligently to choose self-representation, he should be made aware of the dangers and disadvantages of self-representation, so that the record will establish that "he knows what he is doing and his choice is made with eyes open."

In a footnote the Court observed that a state may appoint standby counsel to aid the accused upon his request and to represent the accused if circumstances force termination of his self-representation.

## *Herring* v. *New York*, 422 U.S. 853 (1975)

*Facts:* A New York statute confers upon every judge in a nonjury criminal trial the authority to deny defense counsel the opportunity for final summation of the evidence before rendition of judgment. That statute was attacked as unconstitutional on the ground that it infringed the Sixth Amendment right of the defendant to counsel.

*Question:* Does the challenged statute violate the Sixth Amendment?

*Decision:* Yes. Opinion by Justice Stewart. Vote: 6–3, Burger, Blackmun, and Rehnquist dissenting.

*Reasons:* Past Supreme Court decisions have construed the Sixth Amendment right to counsel to mean that there can be no restrictions upon the functions of counsel in defending a criminal prosecution that are important to the constitutional adversary fact-finding process.

> There can be no doubt that closing argument for the defense is a basic element of the adversary factfinding process in a criminal trial. . . . [It] serves to sharpen and clarify the issues for resolution by the trier of fact. . . . For it is only after all the evidence is in that counsel to the parties are in a position to present their respective versions of the case as a whole. Only then can they argue that inferences to be drawn from all the testimony, and point out the weaknesses of their adversaries' positions. And for the defense, closing argument is the last clear chance to persuade the trier of fact that there may be reasonable doubt of the defendant's guilt.

## *United States* v. *Peltier*, 422 U.S. 531 (1975)

*Facts:* Four months before the decision in *Almeida-Sanchez* v. *United States*, 413 U.S. 266 (1973), Peltier was stopped in his car by roving border-patrol officials acting without a warrant near the Mexican border. Evidence of unlawful possession of marijuana was found in the car trunk. A district court denied Peltier's motion to suppress the evidence and rejected the claim that it was obtained as a result of an illegal search in violation of the Fourth Amendment. The court of appeals reversed on the ground that the rule of *Almeida-Sanchez* should be retroactively applied. (That case held that warrantless automobile searches conducted about twenty-five miles from the Mexican border by border-patrol agents acting without probable cause violated the Fourth Amendment.)

*Question:* Should *Almeida-Sanchez* be applied retroactively to searches preceding its announcement?

*Decision:* No. Opinion by Justice Rehnquist. Vote: 5–4, Douglas, Brennan, Stewart, and Marshall dissenting.

*Reasons:* The exclusionary rule precluding the use of evidence obtained in violation of Fourth Amendment guarantees serves two purposes: First, it deters Fourth Amendment violations. That purpose, however, is not advanced if the challenged official action was taken in good faith. Second, it preserves judicial integrity by refusing, in any way, to sanction willful unconstitutional practices. These purposes would not be served by retroactive application of *Almeida-Sanchez* because the conduct it held unconstitutional had previously been considered legal, and the border-patrol agents who searched Peltier's car acted in good faith in the belief that their actions were legal.

The roving automobile searches at issue in *Almeida-Sanchez* were made in reliance on a federal statute, supported by longstanding administrative regulations and constitutional approval by many lower federal courts. "If the purpose of the exclusionary rule is to deter unlawful police conduct, then evidence obtained from a search should be suppressed only if it can be said that the law enforcement officer had knowledge, or may properly be charged with knowledge, that the search was unconstitutional under the Fourth Amendment."

### *United States* v. *Ortiz*, 422 U.S. 891 (1975)

*Facts:* Without reason to suspect any illegal conduct, border-patrol officers stopped a car at a fixed traffic checkpoint approximately sixty miles from the border between California and Mexico and discovered three illegal aliens. The car owner's conviction for knowingly transporting illegal aliens was reversed on the ground that his being stopped by the border patrol violated the Fourth Amendment because it was not justified by probable cause.

*Question:* Do motor vehicle searches conducted without probable cause by the border patrol at inland traffic checkpoints violate the Fourth Amendment?

*Decision:* Yes. Opinion by Justice Powell. Vote: 9–0.

*Reasons:* In *Almeida-Sanchez* v. *United States*, 413 U.S. 266 (1973), the Court rejected the claim that the strong national interest in controlling illegal immigration plus the practical difficulties of policing the Mexican border justified dispensing with the requirements for both warrant and probable cause for vehicle searches by roving patrols near the border. The issue here is whether the *Almeida-Sanchez* rationale should apply to searches at traffic checkpoints.

The government claimed that such searches are constitutionally distinguishable from roving patrol searches in two respects. First, the discretion of the officers to search particular cars is limited by the location of the checkpoint. Second, searches at checkpoints involve a lesser invasion of privacy than roving patrol searches. The first distinction was viewed as unpersuasive because officers stop and search only a small percentage of cars passing through the checkpoint. Thus, they exercise considerable discretion. The second distinction fails to recognize that motorists whose cars are searched may suffer considerable embarrassment because only a small minority of cars are stopped.

Accordingly, "at traffic checkpoints removed from the border and its functional equivalents, officers may not search private vehicles without consent or probable cause."

### *United States* v. *Brignoni-Ponce*, 422 U.S. 873 (1975)

*Facts:* Roving border-patrol officers stopped an automobile near the Mexican border to question its occupants about their citizenship and immigration status. The sole basis for suspecting any illegality was that the occupants appeared to be of Mexican ancestry. The questioning revealed that the car owner was transporting two illegal aliens. At his subsequent trial for knowingly transporting illegal aliens, the owner unsuccessfully moved to suppress the testimony of and about the two passengers on the ground that it was the fruit of an illegal seizure in violation of the Fourth Amendment.

*Question:* Is the Fourth Amendment violated when roving border-patrol officers stop a vehicle near the border and question its occupants when the only ground for suspecting illegality is that the occupants appear to be of Mexican descent?

*Decision:* Yes. Opinion by Justice Powell. Vote: 9–0.

*Reasons:* The Fourth Amendment applies to all official seizures of the person, including those involving only a brief detention short of an arrest. Such seizures are constitutional only if "reasonable," considering both the public interest and the individual's right to personal secuity free from arbitrary interference by law enforcement officers.

The public interest in preventing illegal immigration across the 2,000-mile Mexican border is strong. It is estimated that 85 percent of the millions of aliens who are in the country illegally are from Mexico. On the other hand, the interference with individual liberty involved when an officer briefly stops a car and questions its occupants is modest. Accordingly, "stops of this sort may be justified on facts that do not amount to the probable cause required for an arrest." In this case, however, the facts did not justify the stop.

In *Terry* v. *Ohio*, 392 U.S. 1 (1968), and *Adams* v. *Williams*, 407 U.S. 143 (1972), the Court concluded that reasonable suspicion that a person was armed and dangerous would justify a limited police search for weapons under the Fourth Amendment. This is the so-called stop and frisk. The reasonable-suspicion test was adopted partly because of practical law enforcement needs. Similarly, considering the strong governmental interest in apprehending illegal aliens,

> the minimal intrusion of a brief stop, and the absence of practical alternatives for policing the border, we hold that when an officer's observations lead him reasonably to suspect that a particular vehicle may contain aliens who are illegally in the country, he may stop the car briefly and investigate the circumstances that provoke suspicion. . . . The officer may question the driver and passengers about their citizenship and immigration status, and he may ask them to explain suspicious circumstances, but any further detention or search must be based on consent or probable cause.

The needs of legitimate law enforcement do not justify eliminating the reasonable-suspicion requirement. However, many factors may be relevant to the determination of its existence in connection with stopping a car in the border area—the character of the area, its proximity to the border, customary patterns of traffic, prior experience with alien traffic, and unusual characteristics of the vehicle or its occupants. Here the only factor relied upon to justify the stop was the apparent Mexican ancestry of the occupants of the vehicle. That factor alone can never establish reasonable suspicion.

> Large numbers of native-born and naturalized citizens have the physical characteristics identified with Mexican ancestry, and even in the border area a relatively small proportion of them are aliens. The likelihood that any given person of Mexican ancestry is an alien is high enough to make Mexican appearance a relevant factor, but standing alone it does not justify stopping all Mexican-Americans to ask if they are aliens.

### *Gerstein* v. *Pugh*, 420 U.S. 103 (1975)

*Facts:* Under Florida law, prosecutors may charge all crimes, except capital offenses, by information, without a prior preliminary hearing and without obtaining leave of court. An individual arrested under an information can be detained for thirty days or more before obtaining a judicial determination of probable cause to believe that he had committed the offense charged. That is, a person charged by information could be detained for a substantial period solely on the decision of a prosecutor.

The Florida law was attacked in federal district court on the ground that the Fourth Amendment prohibition against unreasonable seizures required that all arrested persons charged by information be given an immediate judicial hearing on the question of probable cause. In sustaining the attack, the district court ruled that at the judicial hearing to determine probable cause, the accused was entitled to appointed counsel, to confront and cross-examine adverse witnesses, and to have a transcript made on request. The court of appeals affirmed with minor modifications.

*Questions:* (1) Is a person arrested on an information entitled under the Fourth Amendment to a speedy judicial determination of probable cause prior to extended detention? (2) If so, is the type of adversary hearing ordered by the district court required by the Constitution?

*Decision:* Yes to the first question and no to the second. Opinion by Justice Powell. Vote: 9–0 on the first question and 5–4 on the second, Stewart, Douglas, Brennan, and Marshall dissenting.

*Reasons:* Under the Fourth Amendment, an arrest is justified only upon probable cause,

> defined in terms of facts and circumstances "sufficient to warrant a prudent man in believing that the [suspect] had committed or was committing an offense." . . . To implement the Fourth Amendment's protection against unfounded invasions of liberty and privacy, the Court has required that the existence of probable cause be decided by a neutral and detached magistrate whenever possible. . . . Maximum protection of individual rights could be assured by requiring a magistrate's review of the factual justification prior to any arrest, but such a requirement would constitute an intolerable handicap for legitimate law enforcement.

Thus, the Court has concluded that

> a policeman's on-the-scene assessment of probable cause provides legal justification for arresting a person suspected of crime, and for a brief period of detention to take the administrative steps incident to arrest. Once the suspect is in custody, however, the reasons that justify dispensing with the magistrate's neutral judgment evaporate. There no longer is any danger that the suspect will escape or commit further crimes while the police submit their evidence to a magistrate. And, while the State's reasons for taking summary action subside, the suspect's need for a neutral determination of probable cause increases significantly. The consequences of prolonged detention may be more serious than the interference occasioned by arrest. Pretrial confinement may imperil the suspect's job, interrupt his source of income, and impair his family relationships. . . . When the stakes are this high, the detached judgment of a neutral magistrate is essential if the Fourth Amendment is to furnish meaningful protection from unfounded interference with liberty. Accordingly, we hold that the Fourth Amendment requires a judicial determination of probable cause as a prerequisite to extended restraint on liberty following arrest.

The district court held that the determination of probable cause must be accompanied by the full array of adversary safeguards —counsel, confrontation, cross-examination, and compulsory process for witnesses. These safeguards, however, are not required to insure reliable determinations of whether there is probable cause to detain an arrested person pending further proceedings. Such determinations prior to the issuance of arrest warrants have traditionally been made by magistrates in a "nonadversary proceeding on hearsay and written testimony." Informal procedures are justified because determining probable cause

> does not require the fine resolution of conflicting evidence that a reasonable-doubt or even a preponderance standard demands, and credibility determinations are seldom crucial in deciding whether the evidence supports a reasonable belief in guilt. . . . [Although] confrontation and cross-examination might . . . enhance the reliability of probable cause determinations in some cases . . . [i]n most cases . . . their value would be too slight to justify holding, as a matter of constitutional principle, that these formalities and safeguards designed for trial must also be employed in making the Fourth Amendment determination of probable cause.

## *United States* v. *Bisceglia*, 420 U.S. 141 (1975)

*Facts:* After learning of two $20,000 bank deposits which he suspected represented income not reported for tax purposes, an agent of the Internal Revenue Service issued a "John Doe" summons to the bank calling for the production of books and records that might identify the depositor. The summons was issued pursuant to section 7602 of the Internal Revenue Code. The bank refused to comply, claiming that section 7602 authorizes a summons only when the IRS has already identified the person in whom it is interested. The district court ordered the bank to comply but the court of appeals reversed.

*Question:* Was the "John Doe" summons authorized by section 7602?

*Decision:* Yes. Opinion by Chief Justice Burger. Vote: 7–2, Stewart and Douglas dissenting.

*Reasons:* Section 7601 of the Internal Revenue Code gives the IRS

> a broad mandate to investigate and audit "persons who *may* be liable" for taxes and section 7602 provides the power to "examine any books, papers, records or other data which may be relevant . . . and to summon . . . any person having possession . . . of books of account . . . relevant or material to such inquiry." . . . The purpose of the statutes is not to accuse, but to inquire. Although such investigations unquestionably involve some invasion of privacy, they are essential to our self-reporting system, and the alternatives could well involve far less agreeable invasions of house, business, and records. (Emphasis in original.)

The language of the statutes "is inconsistent with an interpretation that would limit the issuance of summons to investigations which have already focused upon a particular return, a particular named person, or a particular potential tax liability."

The Court added, however, that section 7602 summons power could not be used to conduct "fishing expeditions" and that federal courts should refuse to enforce any summons which went beyond the needs of a legitimate investigation.

## *Mullaney* v. *Wilbur*, 421 U.S. 684 (1975)

*Facts:* Under Maine law, all felonious homicides are punished as murder, unless the defendant proves by a fair preponderance of the evidence that his act was committed in the heat of passion on sudden provocation, in which case it is punished as manslaughter. Murder is punishable by life imprisonment, whereas manslaughter is punishable by a fine not exceeding $1,000 or imprisonment not exceeding twenty years. The constitutionality of the Maine homicide law was challenged under the due process clause of the Fourteenth Amendment on the ground that it failed to require the prosecution to prove the absence of the heat of passion on sudden provocation beyond a reasonable doubt.

*Question:* Does the Maine law of homicide violate due process?

*Decision:* Yes. Opinion by Justice Powell. Vote: 9–0.

*Reasons: In re Winship,* 397 U.S. 358 (1970), held that the due process clause of the Fourteenth Amendment requires that the prosecution prove beyond a reasonable doubt every fact necessary to constitute the crime charged. Maine argued that *Winship* is inapplicable here because the absence of provocation is not an element of the crime of felonious homicide—that is, that failure to prove this element would not justify acquittal, but only a lesser punishment.

To accept that narrow interpretation of *Winship,* however, would be to exalt form over substance. Irrespective of the way that Maine chooses to define the elements of the crime of felonious homicide,

> [t]he fact remains that the consequences resulting from a verdict of murder, as compared with a verdict of manslaughter, differ significantly. Indeed, when viewed in terms of the potential difference in restrictions of personal liberty attendant to each conviction, the distinction established by Maine between murder and manslaughter may be of greater importance than the difference between guilt or innocence for many lesser crimes.

The *Winship* decision rested on the belief that the reliability of verdicts in criminal cases is of the utmost importance. An adverse verdict may cause the accused to be both incarcerated and stigmatized. In addition, the moral force of the criminal law must not be impaired by a standard of proof that leaves people in doubt as to whether or not innocent men are being condemned. The Maine homicide law is inconsistent with the rationale of *Winship* as it

> requires a defendant to establish by a preponderance of the evidence that he acted in the heat of passion on sudden

provocation in order to reduce murder to manslaughter. Under this burden of proof a defendant can be given a life sentence when the evidence indicates that it is *as likely as not* that he deserves a significantly lesser sentence. This is an intolerable result in a society where . . . it is far worse to sentence one guilty only of manslaughter as a murderer than to sentence a murderer for the lesser crime of manslaughter. (Emphasis in original.)

## *Murphy* v. *Florida*, 421 U.S. 794 (1975)

*Facts:* A notorious criminal known as "Murph the Surf" was convicted in Florida state court of robbery. He sought habeas corpus relief claiming that his constitutional right to a fair trial had been denied because members of the jury had learned from news accounts about an earlier felony conviction and certain facts about the robbery charge.

*Question:* Was the defendant denied his constitutional right to a fair trial?

*Decision:* No. Opinion by Justice Marshall. Vote: 8–1, Brennan dissenting.

*Reasons:* "The constitutional standard of fairness requires that a defendant have 'a panel of impartial, indifferent jurors.' Qualified jurors need not, however, be totally ignorant of the facts and issues involved." It is sufficient if a juror can lay aside any preconceived impressions or opinions and render a verdict on the evidence presented in court. Of course, the assurances of a juror that he is equal to this task do not dispose of the issue.

In this case, however, there is no substantial evidence that the jurors who served at the defendant's trial could not lay aside any predisposition to convict. The *voir dire* indicated no hostility on the part of any juror toward the defendant. The news stories about him were largely factual rather than inflammatory and were published seven months before trial. Moreover, only twenty of the seventy-eight potential jurors questioned were excused because they indicated an opinion as to the defendant's guilt. There has been no showing that the setting of the robbery trial was inherently prejudicial or that the jury selection process permitted an inference of actual juror prejudice against the defendant.

*United States* v. *Nobles*, 422 U.S. 225 (1975)

*Facts:* During the trial of Nobles for armed robbery, his defense counsel sought to impeach the credibility of principal witnesses for the prosecution with the testimony of a defense investigator. The investigator was prepared to testify regarding statements he had obtained from the witnesses which were allegedly inconsistent with their testimony at the trial. The federal district court ruled, however, that the investigator could not testify unless a copy of his report relating to the interviews with the witnesses was supplied to the prosecutor. Nobles was convicted after his defense counsel refused to produce the investigator's report. The court of appeals reversed on the grounds that both the Fifth Amendment privilege against self-incrimination and Rule 16 of the Federal Rules of Criminal Procedure (FRCrP) prohibited this disclosure condition from being placed upon the defense investigator's testimony.

*Question:* Was the district court's ruling which prevented the investigator's testimony absent disclosure to the prosecution of the relevant portions of his report appropriate?

*Decision:* Yes. Opinion by Justice Powell. Vote: 8–0. Douglas did not participate.

*Reasons:* "The dual aim of our criminal justice system is 'that guilt shall not escape or innocence suffer.'" The ends of criminal justice would be defeated if judgments were to be founded on a partial and speculative presentation of the facts. Accordingly, "[d]ecisions of this Court repeatedly have recognized the federal judiciary's inherent power to require the prosecution to produce the previously recorded statements of its witnesses so that the defense may get the full benefit of cross-examination and the truth-finding process may be enhanced." Similarly, in this case the production of the defense investigator's report might have substantially enhanced the search for the truth. Thus, its production could properly be compelled by the district court.

The privilege against compulsory self-incrimination was no barrier to producing the report. Quoting from *Couch* v. *United States*, 409 U.S. 322 (1973), the Court stated that "the privilege is a *personal* privilege; it adheres basically to the person, not to information that may incriminate him."

In this instance disclosure of the relevant portions of the defense investigator's report would not impinge on the fundamental values protected by the Fifth Amendment. . . . [Nobles] did not prepare the report, and there is no suggestion that the portions subject to the disclosure order reflected any information that he conveyed to the investigator. . . . Requiring their production from the investigator therefore would not in any sense compel [Nobles] to be a witness against himself or extort communications from him.

Neither did Rule 16 of the FRCrP preclude the district court's ruling. Both the language and history of that rule indicate that its application is limited to pretrial discovery orders. It does not limit the district court's "broad discretion as to evidentiary questions at trial."

Finally, it is claimed that the work-product doctrine of *Hickman* v. *Taylor*, 329 U.S. 495 (1947), protected the investigator's report from disclosure. *Hickman* v. *Taylor* established the general principle that certain materials and documents prepared by an attorney for trial are protected from pretrial discovery. The major purpose of the work-product doctrine is to prevent the adverse effects which would flow from permitting one party to take advantage of his adversary's preparation for trial.

Whatever the scope of the work-product doctrine at trial, in this instance the defense waived any protection he may have had regarding the questioned report by electing to present the investigator as a witness. "[Nobles] can no more advance the work product doctrine to sustain a unilateral testimonial use of work product materials than he could elect to testify in his own behalf and thereafter assert his Fifth Amendment privilege to resist cross-examination on matters reasonably related to those brought out in direct examination."

### *United States* v. *Park*, 421 U.S. 658 (1975)

*Facts:* The president of a large national retail food chain (Acme) and the food chain were charged with violating section 301(k) of the Federal Food, Drug, and Cosmetic Act for allegedly causing interstate food shipments to be exposed to contamination by rodents. Acme pleaded guilty. At the trial of the president he testified that one of his responsibilities was providing sanitary conditions for storage and display of food sold to the public but that he assigned that task to dependable subordinates. Evidence was also adduced showing that the Food and Drug Administration had informed the president of unsanitary conditions in one of Acme's warehouses more than one year before the criminal charges were brought.

The president was convicted after the jury had been instructed that he could be held criminally liable for the contamination by rodents, even if he did not personally participate in permitting that condition to exist, if he had a "responsible relationship" to the problem. The court of appeals reversed on the ground that the instructions to the jury failed to state that criminal liability could attach to the president only if he engaged in wrongful acts of commission or omission.

*Question:* Did the instructions to the jury properly define the standard of criminal liability of corporate officers under the act?

*Decision:* Yes. Opinion by Chief Justice Burger. Vote: 6–3, Stewart, Marshall, and Powell dissenting.

*Reasons:* In *United States v. Dotterweich*, 320 U.S. 277 (1943), the Court noted that the purposes of the act "touch phases of the lives and health of people which, in the circumstances of modern industrialism, are largely beyond self-protection." It observed that the act "dispenses with the conventional requirement for criminal conduct—awareness of some wrongdoing. In the interest of the larger good it puts the burden of acting at hazard upon a person otherwise innocent but standing in responsible relation to a public danger." In *Dotterweich* the Court concluded that under the act an offense was committed "by all who do have . . . a responsible share in the furtherance of the transaction which the statute outlaws."

*Dotterweich* and subsequent cases have established the doctrine

> that in providing sanctions which reach and touch the individuals who execute the corporate mission—and this is by no means necessarily confined to a single corporate agent or employee—the Act imposes not only a positive duty to seek out and remedy violations when they occur but also, and primarily, a duty to implement measures that will insure that violations will not occur. The requirements of foresight and vigilance imposed on responsible corporate agents are beyond question demanding, and perhaps onerous, but they are no more stringent than the public has a right to expect of those who voluntarily assume positions of authority in business enterprises whose services and products affect the health and well-being of the public that supports them. . . . The Act does not . . . make criminal liability turn on "awareness of some wrongdoing" or "conscious fraud."

The failure of the instructions to the jury to require a finding of wrongful action on the part of the president was not error.

The concept of a "reasonable relationship" to, or a "responsible share" in, a violation of the Act indeed imports some measure of blameworthiness; but it is equally clear that the Government establishes a prima facie case when it introduces evidence sufficient to warrant a finding by the trier of the facts that the defendant had, by reason of his position in the corporation, responsibility and authority either to prevent in the first instance, or promptly to correct, the violation complained of, and that he failed to do so.

## *Schick* v. *Reed,* 419 U.S. 256 (1974)

*Facts:* In 1960, the President commuted petitioner Schick's sentence to life imprisonment, subject to the condition that he would not thereafter be eligible for parole. Schick was sentenced to death after conviction by a court-martial for murder, under Article 118 of the Uniform Code of Military Justice.

Several years later, Schick brought suit against the United States Parole Board challenging the constitutionality of the condition placed upon the commutation of his death sentence. Except for this condition, he would have been eligible for parole in 1969. Schick argued that the President's pardon power did not authorize such a condition, and that the decision of the Court in *Furman* v. *Georgia,* 408 U.S. 238 (1972), which voided all pending death sentences, should be retroactively applied to nullify the condition. The district court granted the motion of the parole board for summary judgment, and the court of appeals affirmed.

*Question:* Is the condition attached to Schick's commutation constitutional?

*Decision:* Yes. Opinion by Chief Justice Burger. Vote: 6–3, Marshall, Douglas, and Brennan dissenting.

*Reasons:* Article II, section 2, clause 1, of the Constitution authorizes the President to "grant Reprieves and Pardons for Offenses against the United States except in Cases of Impeachment." The constitutional history of that provision makes clear that it was intended to confer pardon powers resembling those enjoyed by the English crown. At the time of the constitutional convention, it was accepted English law that the king could place conditions upon the exercise of his pardon powers. "In light of the English common law from which such language was drawn, the conclusion is inescapable that the pardoning power was intended to include the power to commute sentences on conditions which do not in themselves offend the Constitution, but which are not specifically provided for by statute." Accordingly, the challenged condition was lawful when imposed in 1960.

The decision of the Court in *Furman* v. *Georgia* has not nullified this condition. It is contended that since *Furman* voided all death sentences and that since the challenged condition could not have been imposed absent Schick's death sentence, then the condition falls with the death sentence. The President, however, has "constitutional power to attach conditions to his commutation of any sentence," not just death sentences. "Thus, even if *Furman* v. *Georgia* applies to the military, a matter which we need not and do not decide, it could not affect a conditional commutation which was granted 12 years earlier."

## Aid to Sectarian Schools and Student Rights

The Court has struggled in recent years with cases requiring application of its three-part test to determine the constitutionality of state aid to sectarian elementary and secondary schools under the establishment clause of the First Amendment. The Court has ruled that to satisfy that clause the aid must have a secular purpose and a primary effect that neither advances nor inhibits religion, and its administration must avoid excessive government entanglement with religion. In applying the test, the Court has held unconstitutional state aid to elementary and secondary parochial schools in the form of (1) salary supplements to school teachers, (2) payments for secular textbooks, (3) tax credits or subsidies to parents of schoolchildren, (4) tuition reimbursement, (5) money to maintain or repair school facilities, and (6) reimbursement for the costs of administering tests and maintaining records required under state law.[8]

Before the Court developed the three-pronged test, however, it had upheld state aid in the form of textbook loans to parochial schoolchildren[9] and free public transportation to and from school.[10] This term, in *Meek* v. *Pittenger*, 421 U.S. 349, the Court appeared to foreclose any other type of state aid to sectarian schools. It suggested that state aid requiring continuing appropriations would be unconsti-

---

[8] See Committee for Public Education and Religious Liberty v. Nyquist, 413 U.S. 756 (1973); Levitt v. Committee for Public Education and Religious Liberty, 413 U.S. 472 (1973); Sloan v. Lemon, 413 U.S. 825 (1973); Lemon v. Kurtzman, 403 U.S. 602 (1971).

[9] Board of Education v. Allen, 392 U.S. 236 (1968).

[10] Everson v. Board of Education, 330 U.S. 1 (1947).

tutional because it would provide opportunities for political divisions along religious lines, a principal evil that the establishment clause was intended to prevent. It seems difficult to conceive of any substantial program of state aid to sectarian schools that could avoid this apparent fourth test to clear the establishment-clause barrier. Textbook-loan and public-transportation programs seem justified under this test only by the principle of stare decisis.[11]

Whether the Court would apply the same strict standards in judging the constitutionality of state aid to religious-affiliated colleges and universities is unclear. In past cases the Court has adopted a more permissive standard of review for aid to such institutions of higher education than for aid to elementary and secondary schools on the theory that religious concerns and effects are less pervasive in institutions of higher education.[12]

For the first time in several terms the Court decided significant cases regarding the constitutional rights of secondary-school students. The last important case in this area was in 1969, when the Court held that high-school principals violated the First Amendment in prohibiting students from wearing black armbands as a symbolic protest against the war in Vietnam.[13] The Court noted that neither students nor teachers "shed their constitutional rights to freedom of speech or expression at the schoolhouse gate."

This term, in a pair of 5–4 decisions written by Justice White, the Court concluded that public-school students are constitutionally entitled to a hearing prior to suspension from school and that they may recover damages against school officials who fail to act in good faith in depriving them of constitutional rights. The Court indicated that school officials would be presumed to have knowledge of the unquestioned constitutional rights of students. The dissenters argued that this rule would unnecessarily discourage persons from volunteering their services on school boards.

---

[11] The decisions of the Court seemingly barring any substantial aid to parochial schools have financial and educational implications for state and local officials with responsibility for public education. In the 1975-76 school term, approximately 3.5 million pupils attended private Catholic elementary and secondary schools. If these schools are forced to close because of a lack of financial support, the cost of educating their students in public schools would be approximately $5 billion annually. In the 1975-76 term, public elementary and secondary schools were educating approximately 45 million pupils at an annual cost of approximately $67 billion. See generally "There's an Unholy Mess in the Churchly Economy," *Fortune*, May 1976.

[12] See Hunt v. McNair, 413 U.S. 734 (1973); Tilton v. Richardson, 403 U.S. 672 (1971).

[13] Tinker v. Des Moines School District, 393 U.S. 503 (1969).

## *Meek* v. *Pittenger*, 421 U.S. 349 (1975)

*Facts:* Pennsylvania provides three types of aid to children attending its nonpublic elementary and secondary schools. First, it lends without charge textbooks acceptable for use in public schools to children attending nonpublic elementary and secondary schools. Second, it provides enrolled students with free "auxiliary services" performed by public-school employees. Those services include counseling, testing, psychological services, speech and hearing therapy, and teaching and related services for exceptional children, remedial students, and the educationally disadvantaged. Third, it lends without charge, directly to the nonpublic schools, instructional materials and equipment useful to the education of their pupils. Pennsylvania's aid to nonpublic schools was challenged on the ground that it violated the establishment clause of the First Amendment, made applicable to the states by the Fourteenth Amendment.

*Question:* Does the challenged Pennsylvania aid to nonpublic elementary and secondary schools violate the establishment clause of the First Amendment?

*Decision:* Yes, except for the lending of textbooks to nonpublic schoolchildren. Opinion by Justice Stewart. Vote: 6–3. Blackmun and Powell joined the plurality opinion. Douglas, Brennan, and Marshall dissented from the conclusion that the aide in the form of textbook loans was constitutional. Burger, White, and Rehnquist dissented from the conclusion that aid in the form of auxiliary services or instructional materials and equipment was unconstitutional.

*Reasons:* The textbook loan program must be upheld on the authority of *Board of Education* v. *Allen*, 392 U.S. 236 (1968). There the Court upheld a New York law which made available to all children the benefits of a general program to lend schoolbooks free of charge. Books were furnished at the request of the pupil and ownership remained, at least technically, in the state. Thus no funds or books were furnished to parochial schools, and the financial benefit was to parents and children, not to schools. Accordingly, the Court concluded that the law did not provide an unconstitutional degree of support for a religious institution. The Pennsylvania textbook loan program is in every material respect identical to the loan program approved in *Allen*.

In determining the constitutionality of the other state aid programs, the Court applied its well-established three-part test: "First, the statute must have a secular legislative purpose. . . . Second, it must have a 'primary effect' that neither advances nor inhibits religion. . . . Third, the statute and its administration must avoid excessive government entanglement with religion." The primary beneficiaries of the instructional material and equipment loan program are sectarian schools because they constitute 75 percent of nonpublic schools in Pennsylvania. In addition, the amount of this aid is "massive," reaching $12 million for the 1972–73 school year. Even though earmarked for secular purposes, when substantial state aid is given to an institution, a substantial portion of whose functions are subsumed in the religious mission, it has the impermissible primary effect of advancing religion. Religion pervades the church-related nonpublic elementary and secondary schools in Pennsylvania. "For this reason . . . direct aid to [such] schools, even though ostensibly limited to wholly neutral, secular instructional material and equipment, inescapably results in the direct and substantial advancement of religious activity . . . and thus constitutes an impermissible establishment of religion."

The provision of auxiliary teaching services violates the establishment clause because to obtain necessary assurances that such services do not advance sectarian purposes would require excessive state entanglement with religion. No matter what subjects state-funded instructors teach, a danger exists that religious doctrine will became intertwined with secular education.

> And a state-subsidized guidance counselor is surely as likely as a state-subsidized chemistry teacher to fail on occasion to separate religious instruction and the advancement of religious beliefs from his secular educational responsibilities.
> The fact that the teachers and counselors providing auxiliary services are . . . public [employees] rather than [employees] of the church-related schools in which they work, does not substantially eliminate the need for continuing surveillance. To be sure, auxiliary services personnel, because not employed by the nonpublic schools, are not directly subject to the discipline of a religious authority. But they are performing important educational services in schools in which education is an integral part of the dominant sectarian mission and in which an atmosphere dedicated to the advancement of religious belief is constantly maintained. . . . The potential for impermissible fostering of religion under these circumstances, although somewhat reduced, is nonetheless present. To be certain that auxiliary teachers remain religiously neutral, as the Constitution demands, the State

would have to impose limitations on the activities of auxiliary personnel and then engage in some form of continuing surveillance to ensure that those restrictions were being followed.

In addition, recurring appropriations would be needed to fund the auxiliary services program. This would provide

> successive opportunities for political fragmentation and division along religious lines, one of the principal evils against which the Establishment Clause was intended to protect. . . . This potential for political entanglement, together with the administrative entanglement which would be necessary to ensure that auxiliary services personnel remain strictly neutral and nonideological when functioning in church-related schools, compels the conclusion that [providing auxiliary services] violates the constitutional prohibition against laws "respecting an establishment of religion."

### *Goss* v. *Lopez*, 419 U.S. 565 (1975)

*Facts:* As authorized by an Ohio statute, several high-school students were summarily suspended from school for up to ten days for alleged misconduct. They brought a class action against the board of education and various school administrators seeking to enjoin the issuance of future suspension orders pursuant to the statute and to compel removal of references to past suspensions from their school records. The students contended that the statute unconstitutionally deprived them of their rights to an education in violation of the due process clause of the Fourteenth Amendment because it did not afford them the opportunity for a hearing of any kind. A three-judge district court declared that the students' suspensions denied them due process of law.

*Question:* Are public-school students constitutionally entitled to a hearing prior to suspension from school, except in emergency situations?

*Decision:* Yes. Opinion by Justice White. Vote: 5–4, Burger, Blackmun, Powell, and Rehnquist dissenting.

*Reasons:* Suspending the students from school deprived them of both "property" and "liberty" entitled to constitutional protection under the due-process clause. Protected interests in property are normally not created by the Constitution but by state statutes or rules entitling individuals to certain benefits. Under Ohio law, the suspended students "plainly had legitimate claims of entitlement to a public education." Having chosen to provide an education, "Ohio may not withdraw that right on grounds of misconduct absent fundamentally fair procedures to determine whether the misconduct has occurred."

Liberty entitled to due process protection includes an individual's right to maintain his good name, reputation, honor, or integrity free from governmental attack.

> School authorities here suspended [the students] from school for periods of up to 10 days based on charges of misconduct. If sustained and recorded, those charges could seriously damage the students' standing with their fellow pupils and their teachers as well as interfere with later opportunities for higher education and employment.

Accordingly, the unilateral suspension unconstitutionally deprived the students of liberty without due process.

The procedures that due process requires to be followed before a student may be suspended depends on an appropriate accommodation of the competing interests involved. At a minimum, past decisions require that the student normally be given notice and an opportunity for a hearing.

> We do not believe that school authorities must be totally free from notice and hearing requirements if their schools are to operate with acceptable efficiency. Students facing temporary suspension have interests qualifying for protection of the Due Process Clause, and due process requires, in connection with a suspension of 10 days or less, that the student be given oral or written notice of the charges against him and, if he denies them, an explanation of the evidence the authorities have and an opportunity to present his side of the story. The clause requires at least these rudimentary precautions against unfair or mistaken findings of misconduct and arbitrary exclusion from school. . . . [H]owever, . . . there are recurring situations in which prior notice and hearing cannot be insisted upon. Students whose presence poses a continuing danger to persons or property or an ongoing threat of disrupting the academic process may be immediately removed from school. In such cases, the necessary notice and rudimentary hearing should follow as soon as practicable.

Due process does not require, moreover,

> that hearings in connection with short suspensions must afford the student the opportunity to secure counsel, to con-

front and cross-examine witnesses supporting the charge or to call his own witnesses to verify his version of the incident. Brief disciplinary suspensions are almost countless. To impose in each such case even truncated trial type procedures might well overwhelm administrative facilities in many places and, by diverting resources, cost more than it would save in educational effectiveness. Moreover, further formalizing the suspension process and escalating its formality and adversary nature may not only make it too costly as a regular disciplinary tool but also destroy its effectiveness as part of the teaching process.

## *Wood* v. *Strickland,* 420 U.S. 308 (1975)

*Facts:* After expulsion from school for violating a school regulation prohibiting the use or possession of intoxicating beverages, several high-school students brought suit for compensatory damages against members of the school board and school administrators under 42 U.S.C. 1983. They alleged, *inter alia,* a denial of their constitutional rights to substantive due process because the judgment that they violated the school regulation lacked evidentiary support. After trial, the federal district court directed verdicts for the school officials on the ground that they were immune from section 1983 damage suits absent proof that they maliciously violated constitutional rights, which was lacking in this case. Reversing the district court, the court of appeals ruled that (1) compensatory damages could be recovered if the defendants failed to act in good faith and (2) the students' constitutional rights to substantive due process were violated.

*Questions:* (1) Was the court of appeals correct in ruling that school board members are immune from section 1983 damage suits only if their challenged actions were taken in good faith? (2) Was the court of appeals warranted in finding a violation of substantive due process?

*Decision:* Yes to the first question and no to the second. Opinion by Justice White. Vote: 5–4, Powell, Burger, Blackmun, and Rehnquist dissenting.

*Reasons:* Section 1983, on the face of it, authorizes damage suits against every person who, acting under color of state law, violates another's constitutional rights. In *Tenney* v. *Brandhove,* 341 U.S. 367 (1951) and *Pierson* v. *Ray,* 386 U.S. 547 (1967), however, the Court concluded that section 1983 was not intended to abolish wholesale common-law immunities for public officials. Common-law tradition and strong reasons of public policy lead to the conclusion that under section 1983 school board members are immune from liability for damages if their challenged actions were taken in good faith.

> Liability for damages for every action which is found subsequently to have been violative of a student's constitutional rights and to have caused compensable injury would unfairly impose upon the school decisionmaker the burden of mistakes made in good faith in the course of exercising his discretion within the scope of his official duties. School board members, among other duties, must judge whether there have been violations of school regulations and, if so, the appropriate sanctions for the violations. . . . The imposition of monetary costs for mistakes which were not unreasonable in the light of all the circumstances would undoubtedly deter even the most conscientious school decisionmaker from exercising his judgment independently, forcefully, and in a manner best serving the long-term interest of the school and the students. The most capable candidates for school board positions might be deterred from seeking office if heavy burdens upon their private resources from monetary liability were a likely prospect during their tenure.

Good faith, however, requires that a school officer act

> sincerely and with a belief that he is doing right, but an act violating a student's constitutional rights can be no more justified by ignorance or disregard of settled, indisputable law on the part of one entrusted with supervision of students' daily lives than by the presence of actual malice. To be entitled to a special exemption from the categorical remedial language of section 1983 in a case in which his action violated a student's constitutional rights, a school board member, who has voluntarily undertaken the task of supervising the operation of the school and the activities of the students, must be held to a standard of conduct based not only on permissible intentions, but also on knowledge of the basic, unquestioned constitutional rights of his charges. . . . Therefore, in the specific context of school discipline, we hold that a school board member is not immune from liability for damages under section 1983 if he knew or reasonably should have known that the action he took within his sphere of official responsibility would violate the constitutional rights of the student affected, or if he took the action with the malicious intention to cause a deprivation of constitutional rights or other injury to the student.

The conclusion of the court of appeals that the decision to expel the students lacked evidentiary support rested upon an erroneous interpretation of the school regulation. It interpreted the term "intoxicating beverages" as synonymous with the definition of "intoxicating liquor" under state statutes. That definition restricts the term to beverages with an alcoholic content exceeding 5 percent by weight. However, the record clearly shows that the school regulation was intended to cover all beverages containing alcohol. When so construed, there was evidence to support the charge that the regulation had been violated. Accordingly, the judgment of the court of appeals on the evidentiary question must be reversed.

## Civil Rights and Civil Liberties

The significant decisions of the Court concerning civil rights and civil liberties covered a broad spectrum of issues. As was true of its 1973–74 term, the attitude of the Court toward civil liberties was mixed. It seemed sympathetic to First Amendment claims of freedom of the press, while refusing to extend the concept of "state action" in a way that would subject numerous corporations to provisions of the Constitution that restrict governmental action.

The media were successful in advancing the First Amendment as a barrier to a suit for invasion of privacy and a prosecution for carrying an advertisement about abortion clinics. In *Cox Broadcasting Corp.* v. *Cohn*, 420 U.S. 469, the Court ruled that a state's interest in protecting privacy could not constitutionally authorize a civil suit against the press for broadcasting the name of a rape victim that had been revealed in court. In *Bigelow* v. *Virginia*, 421 U.S. 809, the Court held that a Virginia criminal statute, as applied to the owner of a newspaper which carried advertisements informing Virginia residents where legal abortions could be obtained in New York, violated the First Amendment.[14]

The Court continued a trend begun in recent terms by narrowing the concept of "state action" for purposes of the Fourteenth Amendment. That amendment prohibits a state, *inter alia*, from depriving persons of life, liberty, or property without due process of law. In many cases, the issue is raised of whether action taken by a private organization is sufficiently tied to the state to warrant application of Fourteenth Amendment restrictions on state action. Impelled partly

---

[14] This decision may signal a significant change in the Court's treatment of so-called commercial speech under the First Amendment. See "The Supreme Court, 1974 Term," *Harvard Law Review*, vol. 89 (November 1975), p. 111.

by a concern to eliminate racial discrimination root and branch, the pattern of decisions of the Court until 1970 was to find state action whenever it was claimed.[15] Beginning with its decision in *Evans* v. *Abney*, 396 U.S. 435 (1970), however, the Court has adopted a less expansive view of the state action doctrine.[16] In 1972, the Court ruled that the racially discriminatory practices of a private club holding a state-issued liquor license did not constitute state action.[17] In *Lloyd Corp.* v. *Tanner*, 407 U.S. 551 (1972), the Court concluded that a privately owned shopping center is not prohibited by the First Amendment from barring the distribution of handbills on its property.[18] This term, in *Jackson* v. *Metropolitan Edison Co.*, 419 U.S. 345, the Court held that a state-regulated private utility's termination of electrical service did not constitute state action.

The Court also stepped back from earlier decisions striking down state laws on the ground that they burdened interstate travel unconstitutionally.[19] The basic rationale for these holdings was that the right of interstate travel bars a state from denying benefits or rights to new bona fide state residents. However, in *Sosna* v. *Iowa*, 419 U.S. 393, the Court upheld a state statute requiring one year's residence before a divorce action can be brought.

Obscenity issues reached the Court in two cases. Resting on narrow procedural grounds, the Court ruled in *Southeastern Promotions, Ltd.* v. *Conrad*, 420 U.S. 546, that a municipality improperly denied the use of its theater for the showing of the rock musical *Hair*. The Court also held unconstitutional a city ordinance prohibiting drive-in movie theaters from exhibiting films containing nudity in *Erznoznik* v. *City of Jacksonville*, 422 U.S. 205.

In recent terms the Court has several times addressed the issue of the due process rights of debtors to prevent the seizure of goods

---

[15] See, for example, Terry v. Adams, 345 U.S. 461 (1953); Shelley v. Kramer, 334 U.S. 1 (1948); Burton v. Wilmington Parking Authority, 365 U.S. 715 (1961); Evans v. Newton, 382 U.S. 296 (1966); Reitman v. Mulkey, 387 U.S. 369 (1967).

[16] There the Court concluded that the following action taken by a state court did not impermissibly involve the state in racial discrimination: After determining that a city could not operate a racially segregated public park as stipulated in a will devising the property, the Court ruled that instead of striking the segregation requirement from the will the property should be returned to the decedent's heirs. Compare Shelley v. Kramer, 334 U.S. 1 (1948).

[17] Moose Lodge No. 107 v. Irvis, 407 U.S. 163 (1972).

[18] Compare, Food Employees Union v. Logan Valley Plaza, 391 U.S. 308 (1968); Marsh v. Alabama, 326 U.S. 501 (1946).

[19] See, for example, Shapiro v. Thompson, 394 U.S. 618 (1969); Dunn v. Blumstein, 405 U.S. 330 (1972); Memorial Hospital v. Maricopa County, 415 U.S. 250 (1974).

sold on credit. In *Fuentes* v. *Shevin*, 407 U.S. 67 (1972), the Court indicated that a debtor was entitled to notice and a hearing to establish the probable validity of the creditor's underlying claim before his goods could be seized, even temporarily, pending final judgment. In 1974, however, the Court narrowly construed *Fuentes* and concluded that a debtor's goods might be seized without notice or hearing if certain procedural safeguards existed.[20] This term the Court seemed to reaffirm the spirit of the *Fuentes* decision in striking down a Georgia statute permitting pretrial garnishment of bank accounts without notice or hearing to the alleged debtor.

In a case given national publicity, *O'Connor* v. *Donaldson*, 422 U.S. 563, the Court expanded the rights of the mentally ill. It ruled that a state may not confine without treatment the nondangerous mentally ill who are capable of living safely outside confinement. The Court specifically reserved decision on these more difficult questions, however: whether dangerous mentally ill persons have a right to treatment if confined by the state; whether a state may confine the nondangerous mentally ill for the purpose of treatment; and whether a state may justify confining a person who is mentally ill on the grounds that confinement is necessary to prevent injury to the public or for the person's own safety.

In rejecting First Amendment claims of an organization which had opposed the Vietnam War, the Court gave a liberal interpretation of the congressional power to investigate. Specifically at issue in *Eastland* v. *U.S. Servicemen's Fund*, 421 U.S. 491, was whether the speech or debate clause, Article I, section 6, clause 1, immunized the members of a Senate subcommittee from a suit challenging the constitutionality of a subpoena that the subcommittee had issued during its investigation into subversive activities. The subpoena, which sought the financial records of the organization, was allegedly issued to harass the organization and deter it from exercising its rights of free speech and association. Refusing to inquire into the motives of the subcommittee, the Court concluded that the act of issuing an investigative subpoena, relevant to a subject over which Congress might legitimately legislate, falls within the protection of the speech or debate clause. The tone of the decision stood in contrast to a 1957 opinion by Chief Justice Warren in which he wrote: "We have no doubt that there is no congressional power to expose for the sake of exposure." [21]

---

[20] Mitchell v. W. T. Grant Co., 416 U.S. 600 (1974).
[21] Watkins v. United States, 354 U.S. 178, 200 (1957).

## Cox Broadcasting Corp. v. Cohn, 420 U.S. 469 (1975)

*Facts:* The father of a rape victim who died after the attack brought suit in Georgia state court against a television station, claiming that his right of privacy had been invaded by television broadcasts revealing the name of his deceased daughter. One of the station's reporters obtained the name by examining the indictments of six youths who were charged with the crime. The indictments were public court records.

Relying on a state criminal statute making it a misdemeanor to publish or broadcast the name or identity of a rape victim, the Georgia Supreme Court ruled that the father had made a compensable tort claim for invasion of privacy. It rejected the contention of the broadcaster that the First Amendment's protection of the press prohibited the lawsuit.

*Question:* Does the First Amendment prohibit a state from imposing sanctions on the accurate publication of a rape victim's name which was publicly revealed in connection with the prosecution of the crime?

*Decision:* Yes. Opinion by Justice White. Vote: 8–1, Rehnquist dissenting.

*Reasons:* It must be recognized that this "century has experienced a strong tide running in favor of the so-called right of privacy." Georgia contends that this right permits a state to protect an individual's zone of privacy from intrusion by the press. Although the consideration of privacy is strong, in this case it directly confronts the constitutional freedoms of speech and press. The broadcaster argued "that the press may not be made criminally or civilly liable for publishing information that is neither false nor misleading but absolutely accurate, however damaging it may be to reputation or individual sensibilities." This broad issue, however, need not be addressed in this case. The narrow question here is "whether the State may impose sanctions on the accurate publication of the name of a rape victim obtained from public records—more specifically, from judicial records which are maintained in connection with a public prosecution and which themselves are open to public inspection."

The news media have a great responsibility

> to report fully and accurately the proceedings of government, and official records and documents open to the public are the basic data of governmental operations. Without the

information provided by the press most of us and many of our representatives would be unable to vote intelligently or to register opinions on the administration of government generally. With respect to judicial proceedings in particular, the function of the press serves to guarantee the fairness of trials and to bring to bear the beneficial effects of public scrutiny upon the administration of justice.

In deference to these considerations, the

> prevailing law of invasion of privacy generally recognizes that the interests of privacy fade when the information involved already appears on the public record. . . .
>
> By placing the information in the public domain on official court records, the State must be presumed to have concluded that the public interest was thereby being served. . . . The freedom of the press to publish that information appears to us to be of critical importance to our type of government in which the citizenry is the final judge of the proper conduct of public business. In preserving that form of government the First and Fourteenth Amendments command nothing less than that the States may not impose sanctions for the publication of truthful information contained in official court records open to public inspection.

### *Bigelow* v. *Virginia,* 421 U.S. 809 (1975)

*Facts:* Bigelow's newspaper carried an advertisement informing Virginia residents where legal abortions in New York could be obtained. On the basis of that advertisement, Bigelow was convicted of violating a Virginia statute prohibiting the sale of any publication which "encourage[s] . . . the procuring of an abortion." He challenged the constitutionality of his conviction on the ground that the Virginia statute violated his First Amendment rights of free speech and press.

*Question:* Were Bigelow's First Amendment rights unconstitutionally abridged by the challenged Virginia statute?

*Decision:* Yes. Opinion by Justice Blackmun. Vote: 7–2, Rehnquist and White dissenting.

*Reasons:* It is argued that the First Amendment guarantees of speech and press are totally inapplicable to paid commercial advertisements. That position was rejected by the Court in *Pittsburgh Press Co.* v. *Pittsburgh Commission on Human Relations,* 413 U.S. 376

(1973). The type of information that the advertisement conveys, however, does affect the extent of its protection under the First Amendment against countervailing state interests.

In this case, the advertisement contained factual information, clearly of interest to the public, as to where one could obtain legal abortions in New York. The advertisement

> conveyed information of potential interest and value to a diverse audience—not only to readers possibly in need of the services offered, but also to those with a general curiosity about, or genuine interest in, the subject matter or the law of another State and its development, and to readers seeking reform in Virginia. . . . [Moreover], [t]he Virginia Legislature could not have regulated the advertiser's activity in New York, and obviously could not have proscribed the activity in that State. . . . A State does not acquire power or supervision over the internal affairs of another State merely because the welfare and health of its own citizens may be affected when they travel to that State. It may seek to disseminate information so as to enable its citizens to make better informed decisions when they leave. But it may not, under the guise of exercising internal police powers, bar a citizen of another State from disseminating information about an activity that is legal in that State.

Nevertheless, Virginia claims that the challenged statute can be justified as a measure to protect its citizens from the inadequate medical care commonly associated with commercially operated abortion-referral agencies in New York. The rationale of that argument, however, would permit that state to proscribe

> a wide variety of national publications or interstate newspapers carrying advertisements similar to the one that appeared in Bigelow's newspaper or containing articles on the general subject matter to which the advertisement referred. . . . Other States might do the same. The burdens thereby imposed on publications would impair, perhaps severely, their proper functioning.

Any interest that Virginia had in prohibiting Bigelow's advertisement was insufficient to outweigh the First Amendment interests which were infringed.

### *O'Connor* v. *Donaldson*, 422 U.S. 563 (1975)

*Facts:* In 1957, Donaldson was civilly committed to a Florida state hospital as a mental patient on the ground that he suffered from "paranoid schizophrenia." For fifteen years he was involuntarily confined despite clear evidence that he posed no danger to others or to himself during that period. Donaldson's confinement, moreover, was merely enforced custodial care and not a program designed to treat his alleged illness. He brought suit for damages against his hospital superintendent under 42 U.S.C. 1983, alleging that the superintendent had unconstitutionally refused to permit his release from the hospital. The suit was based on the theory that a state may not involuntarily confine a nondangerous person who is mentally ill without treatment. A jury returned a verdict for Donaldson and awarded damages of $38,500. The court of appeals affirmed.

*Question:* May a state constitutionally confine without treatment a nondangerous, mentally ill person who is capable of surviving safely in freedom by himself or with the help of willing and responsible family members or friends?

*Decision:* No. Opinion by Justice Stewart. Vote: 9–0.

*Reasons:* In this case, there is no need

> to decide whether mentally ill persons dangerous to themselves or to others have a right to treatment upon compulsory confinement by the State, or whether the State may compulsorily confine a nondangerous, mentally ill individual for the purpose of treatment. . . . We [also] need not decide whether, when, or by what procedures, a mentally ill person may be confined by the State on any of the grounds which, under contemporary statutes, are generally advanced to justify involuntary confinement of such a person—to prevent injury to the public, to ensure his own survival or safety, or to alleviate or cure his illness.

The narrow issue here is whether a finding of mental illness alone can justify state custodial detention of an individual against his will.

> [T]here is . . . no constitutional basis for confining such persons involuntarily if they are dangerous to no one and can live safely in freedom.
>   May the State confine the mentally ill merely to ensure them a living standard superior to that they enjoy in the private community? That the State has a proper interest in providing care and assistance to the unfortunate goes without saying. But the mere presence of mental illness does not disqualify a person from preferring his home to the comforts of an institution. Moreover, while the State may arguably

confine a person to save him from harm, incarceration is rarely if ever a necessary condition for raising the living standards of those capable of surviving safely in freedom, on their own or with the help of family or friends.

The Court, however, remanded the case for a determination of whether the hospital superintendent was protected from the damage award by the doctrine of qualified immunity for state officials under section 1983. As that doctrine was enunciated in *Wood* v. *Strickland*, 420 U.S. 308 (1975), the superintendent was liable for damages under that statute only if he

> "knew or reasonably should have known that the action he took within his sphere of official responsibility would violate the constitutional rights of [Donaldson], or if he took the action with the malicious intention to cause a deprivation of constitutional rights or other injury to [Donaldson]."

### *Jackson* v. *Metropolitan Edison Company*, 419 U.S. 345 (1974)

*Facts:* Without affording notice, a hearing, or an opportunity to pay amounts due, a privately owned and operated utility company terminated its service to a customer because of alleged delinquency in payments. The company held a certificate of public convenience issued by the state of Pennsylvania. Seeking damages and injunctive relief, the customer brought suit against the utility under 42 U.S.C. 1983, alleging that the termination unconstitutionally deprived her of property without due process of law. (Section 1983 authorizes suits against any person who, under color of state law, violates another's constitutional rights.) The customer argued that she had a property interest, by virtue of state law, in reasonably continuous electrical service to her home and that the termination constituted "state action" because it was specifically allowed by a provision in the utility's tariff filed with the state public utilities commission.

*Question:* Did the private utility's termination of electrical service constitute "state action" for purposes of the Fourteenth Amendment?

*Decision:* No. Opinion by Justice Rehnquist. Vote: 6–3, Douglas, Brennan, and Marshall dissenting.

*Reasons:* The Fourteenth Amendment provides in part that no state shall "deprive any person of life, liberty, or property without due process of law." It was established in *The Civil Rights Cases*, 109 U.S. 3 (1883), that this clause provides protection against state action, but not against private conduct. To determine into which category particular conduct falls requires a careful sifting of all the facts.

Here the challenged action was taken by a utility subject to extensive state regulation. But the mere fact that "a business is subject to state regulation does not by itself convert its action into that of the State for purposes of the Fourteenth Amendment." There must be "a sufficiently close nexus between the State and the challenged action of the regulated entity so that the action of the latter may be fairly treated as that of the State itself."

It was argued that such a nexus exists because the private utility performed a public function traditionally associated with state sovereignty and the state specifically authorized and approved the utility's termination practices. The former argument must be rejected because under state law neither the state nor its municipalities have any obligation to furnish utility services. The latter argument fails because the state public utilities commission never specifically approved the challenged termination practices; it merely failed to disapprove them when the utility filed its general tariff. This type of approval by a state utility commission, "where [it] has not put its own weight on the side of the proposed practice by ordering it, does not transmute a practice initiated by the utility . . . into 'state' action." In this case, the failure of the commission to overturn the utility's termination practices reflected only a determination that state law did not prohibit such practices. The utility's exercise of the choice allowed by state law where the initiative comes from it and not from the state "does not make its action in doing so 'state action' for purposes of the Fourteenth Amendment."

Accordingly, the state was not sufficiently involved with the utility's termination of the customer's service to attribute that termination to the state under the Fourteenth Amendment.

### Sosna v. Iowa, 419 U.S. 393 (1975)

*Facts:* One month after moving from New York to Iowa, a wife filed a petition for divorce in Iowa state court. The petition was dismissed on the ground that an Iowa statute requires residence of one year before a divorce action may be maintained. Seeking declaratory and injunctive relief, the wife brought a class action in federal district court challenging the constitutionality of the one-year durational residency requirement for invoking Iowa's divorce jurisdiction. She argued that the statutory requirement placed an unconstitutional burden on the right of interstate travel and violated her due process right of access to divorce courts. A federal district court decision rejecting her claims was appealed to the Supreme Court. When the Court heard the case, however, the wife had resided in Iowa for more than one year and had obtained a divorce in New York. The Court was thus also faced with the question of whether the case was moot.

*Questions:* (1) Was the class action moot because the wife had satisfied the Iowa durational residency requirement and obtained a divorce elsewhere when the case reached the Supreme Court? (2) Is Iowa's challenged one-year durational residency requirement constitutional?

*Decision:* No to the first question and yes to the second. Vote: 6–3, White, Marshall, and Brennan dissenting.

*Reasons:* "If [the wife] had sued only on her own behalf, both the fact that she now satisfied the one-year residency requirement and the fact that she has obtained a divorce elsewhere would make this case moot and require dismissal." However, since the case was certified as a class action, the class of unnamed persons acquired a legal status separate from the wife. This "factor significantly affects the mootness determination."

Although Iowa officials

> might not again enforce the Iowa durational residency requirement against [the wife], it is clear that they will enforce it against those persons in the class [she] sought to represent and which the District Court certified. In this sense the case before us is one in which state officials will undoubtedly continue to enforce the challenged statute and yet, because of the passage of time, no single challenger will remain subject to its restrictions for the period necessary to see such a lawsuit to its conclusion.

In class action suits such as this, in which the controversy would inevitably become moot as to the named plaintiffs before full appellate review but remains very much alive for the unnamed plaintiffs, the case is not inexorably rendered moot when the controversy as to the named plaintiffs is resolved.

It is claimed that the durational residency requirement unconstitutionally burdens interstate travel. Prior Supreme Court cases have struck down durational residency requirements which absolutely denied a benefit when the denial was justified on the basis of budgetary or record-keeping considerations. In this case, in contrast, the durational residency requirement delayed but did not foreclose the wife's opportunity to obtain an Iowa divorce. In addition, the reasons for the durational residency requirement transcend budgetary or administration considerations.

A decree of divorce is of concern to both spouses as well as to the state. It may include a settlement of property rights and provisions for the custody of minor children and their support. "With consequences of such moment riding on a divorce decree issued by its courts, Iowa may insist that one seeking to initiate such a proceeding have the modicum of attachment to the State required here."

> Such a requirement additionally furthers the State's parallel interests in both avoiding officious intermeddling in matters in which another State has a paramount interest, and in minimizing the susceptibility of its own divorce decrees to collateral attack. A State such as Iowa may quite reasonably decide that it does not wish to become a divorce mill for unhappy spouses who have lived there as short a time as [the wife] had when she commenced her action in the state court after having long resided elsewhere.

In addition, a state has no authority to grant a divorce to a spouse not actually domiciled there. If a finding of domicile is made in ex parte divorce proceedings, the divorce decree may not be binding on other states which determine by cogent evidence that domicile was lacking.

> For that reason, the State asked to enter such a decree is entitled to insist that the putative divorce plaintiff satisfy something more than the bare minimum of constitutional requirements before a divorce may be granted. The State's decision to exact a one-year residency requirement as a matter of policy is therefore buttressed by a quite permissible inference that this requirement not only effectuates state substantive policy but likewise provides a greater safeguard against successful collateral attack than would a requirement of bona fide residence alone. . . . This is precisely the sort of determination that a State in the exercise of its domestic relations jurisdiction is entitled to make.

The strong state policies behind the durational residency requirement justify any consequent incidental burden placed on the right of interstate travel.

It is also argued that the requirement unconstitutionally deprived the wife of access to Iowa's divorce courts in violation of due process.

That access was only delayed, however, not entirely denied, "and the delay which attends the enforcement of the one-year durational residency requirement is, for the reasons previously stated, consistent with the provisions of the United States Constitution."

## *North Georgia Finishing, Inc.* v. *Di-Chem, Inc.,* 419 U.S. 601 (1975)

*Facts:* A Georgia statute authorizes a plaintiff to garnish the defendant's property before judgment if he makes a conclusory affidavit before a court clerk stating the amount claimed from the defendant and that he has reason to believe that he would lose all or part of that amount absent garnishment and files a bond in twice the amount claimed. The defendant may dissolve the garnishment by filing a bond conditioned to pay any final judgment up to the amount claimed. A defendant corporation whose bank account was garnished challenged the constitutionality of the Georgia law on the ground that it violated the due process clause of the Fourteenth Amendment.

*Question:* Is Georgia's garnishment procedure unconstitutional?

*Decision:* Yes. Opinion by Justice White. Vote: 6–3, Burger, Blackmun, and Rehnquist dissenting.

*Reasons:* In *Fuentes* v. *Shevin,* 407 U.S. 67 (1972),

> the Court held invalid the Florida and Pennsylvania replevin statutes which permitted a secured installment seller to repossess the goods sold, without notice or hearing and without judicial order or supervision, but with the help of the sheriff operating under a writ issued by the clerk of the court at the behest of the seller. That the debtor was deprived of only the use and possession of the property, and perhaps only temporarily, did not put the seizure beyond scrutiny under the Due Process Clause. . . . Because the official seizures had been carried out without notice and without opportunity for a hearing or other safeguard against mistaken repossession, they were held to be in violation of the Fourteenth Amendment.

The Georgia statute suffers the same defects as the statutes held unconstitutional in *Fuentes.* "[A] bank account, surely a form of property, was impounded and, absent a bond, put totally beyond use during the pendency of the litigation on the alleged debt, all by a writ of garnishment issued by a court clerk without notice or opportunity for an early hearing and without participation by a judicial officer."

The Court also noted that the challenged statute lacked the saving characteristics of a Louisiana sequestration statute upheld in *Mitchell v. W. T. Grant Co.*, 416 U.S. 600 (1974). That statute

> permitted the seller-creditor holding a vendor's lien to secure a writ of sequestration and, having filed a bond, to cause the sheriff to take possession of the property at issue. The writ, however, was issuable only by a judge upon the filing of an affidavit going beyond mere conclusory allegations and clearly setting out the facts entitling the creditor to sequestration. The Louisiana law also expressly entitled the debtor to an immediate hearing after seizure and to dissolution of the writ absent proof by the creditor of the grounds on which the writ was issued.

## *Eastland* v. *U.S. Servicemen's Fund*, 421 U.S. 491 (1975)

*Facts:* In 1970, the Senate Subcommittee on Internal Security, of which Senator James Eastland (Democrat, Mississippi), was chairman, was given broad authority by the Senate to investigate the operation and enforcement of the Internal Security Act of 1950. In particular, the subcommittee was directed to investigate subversive activities that might be conducted by persons who may be under the control of foreign goverments. Pursuant to its mandate, the subcommittee began investigating the United States Servicemen's Fund, Inc. (USSF), an organization which attempted to communicate to servicemen its attitudes about the Vietnam War. During its investigation, the subcommittee issued a *subpoena duces tecum* to a bank where USSF had an account, commanding the bank to produce its records pertaining to that account. USSF brought suit against Chairman Eastland, eight other senators, and the chief counsel to the subcommittee, seeking to enjoin implementation of the subpoena. It claimed that the subpoena was issued for the unconstitutional purpose of harassing and deterring USSF in its exercise of First Amendment rights of free speech and association; and that disclosure of its bank records would cause a substantial reduction in private financial contributions to the organization. The defendants sought dismissal of the suit on the ground that their challenged action was immune from judicial scrutiny under the speech or debate clause of the Constitution, Article I, section 6, clause 1.

*Question:* Were the senators and the chief counsel immune from suit under the speech or debate clause?

*Decision:* Yes. Opinion by Chief Justice Burger. Vote: 8–1, Douglas dissenting.

*Reasons:* The purpose of the speech or debate clause is to insure the independence of Congress in performing its legislative function. The Court has held that the clause protects members of Congress from litigation, either civil or criminal, for conduct performed within the "sphere of legislative activity." Activity falls within the legitimate legislative sphere if it is

> an integral part of the deliberative and communicative processes by which Members participate in committee and House proceedings with respect to the consideration and passage or rejection of proposed legislation or with respect to other matters which the Constitution places within the jurisdiction of either House. . . . The power to investigate and to do so through compulsory process plainly falls within that definition. This Court has often noted that the power to investigate is inherent in the power to make laws because "[a] legislative body cannot legislate wisely or effectively in the absence of information respecting the conditions which the legislation is intended to affect or change." To conclude that the power of inquiry is other than an integral part of the legislative process would be a miserly reading of the Speech or Debate Clause in derogation of the integrity of the legislative process.

The challenged activity in this case was in furtherance of a legitimate task of Congress. The subpoena was issued pursuant to an investigation into subversive activity, a subject over which Congress might legitimately legislate. "Inquiry into the sources of funds used to carry on activities suspected by a subcommittee of Congress to have a potential for undermining the morale of the armed forces is within the legitimate legislative sphere."

Accordingly, the speech or debate clause provides absolute immunity for the senators in their issuance of the subpoena. The chief counsel is also protected by that immunity because the Court in *Gravel* v. *United States,* 408 U.S. 606 (1972), stated that "the day-to-day work of such aides is so critical to Members' performance that they must be treated as [the Members'] alter egos" for purposes of the clause.

### *Erznoznik* v. *City of Jacksonville*, 422 U.S. 205 (1975)

*Facts:* A manager of a drive-in movie theater brought suit challenging the constitutionality of a city ordinance prohibiting the exhibition by a drive-in theater of films containing nudity if its screen is visible from a public street or place. He claimed that the ordinance was invalid on its face as a clear violation of the First Amendment protection of free speech.

*Question:* Does the challenged ordinance violate the First Amendment?

*Decision:* Yes. Opinion by Justice Powell. Vote: 6–3, Burger, White, and Rehnquist dissenting.

*Reasons:* It was conceded that the ordinance "sweeps far beyond the permissible restraints on obscenity." Nevertheless, three basic arguments were advanced to justify its impingement on the First Amendment.

First, it was claimed that a city may protect its citizens against unwilling exposure to materials that may be offensive.

> But when the government, acting as censor, undertakes selectively to shield the public from some kinds of speech on the ground that they are more offensive than others, the First Amendment strictly limits its power. . . . Such selective restrictions have been upheld only when the speaker intrudes on the privacy of the home, . . . or the degree of captivity makes it impractical for the unwilling viewer or auditor to avoid exposure.

In the absence of these strong privacy interests, however, the burden normally falls upon the viewer to avoid offending his sensibilities by averting his eyes.

The effect of the challenged ordinance

> is to deter drive-in theaters from showing movies containing any nudity, however innocent or even educational. . . . This discrimination cannot be justified as a means of preventing significant intrusions on privacy. The ordinance seeks only to keep these films from being seen from public streets and places where the offended viewer readily can avert his eyes. . . . Thus, we conclude that the limited privacy interest of persons on the public streets cannot justify this censorship of otherwise protected speech on the basis of its content.

Second, the city contended that the ordinance represents a proper exercise of its police power to protect children. If that is its purpose, however, the ordinance sweeps far too broadly. "[I]t would bar a film containing a picture of a baby's buttocks, the nude body of a war victim, or scenes from a culture in which nudity is indigenous. The ordinance also might prohibit newsreel scenes of the opening of an art exhibit as well as shots of bathers on a beach."

Third, the ordinance was claimed to be justified as a traffic regulation on the theory that nudity on a drive-in movie screen distracts motorists. However,

> by singling out movies containing even the most fleeting and innocent glimpses of nudity the legislative classification is strikingly underinclusive. There is no reason to think that a wide variety of other scenes in the customary screen diet, ranging from soap opera to violence, would be any less distracting to the passing motorist.

Earlier cases have established the principle that the government lacks power to restrict expression because of its content, even through the mechanism of a traffic regulation, unless clear reasons justify this discrimination. No such reasons have been advanced in this case.

### *Southeastern Promotions, Ltd.* v. *Conrad*, 420 U.S. 546 (1975)

*Facts:* A promoter of theatrical productions was denied a request to lease a Chattanooga municipal theater for the purpose of showing the controversial rock musical *Hair*. The denial was made on the ground that the production would not be "in the best interests of the community." The promoter brought suit to enjoin the city theater's board of directors from refusing to grant the lease on the ground, *inter alia*, that its action constituted an unconstitutional prior restraint on free speech.

*Question:* Did the rejection of the promoter's application to use the municipal theater impose a prior restraint on free speech, effected under a system lacking constitutionally required minimal procedural safeguards?

*Decision:* Yes. Opinion by Justice Blackmun. Vote: 5–4, Burger, Douglas, White, and Rehnquist dissenting.

*Reasons:* In a long series of cases, the Court has condemned unbounded actions taken by public officials which denied individuals the use of a public forum to exercise free speech. The Court has reasoned that the exercise of such authority must be constrained by "precise and clear standards" because "the danger of censorship and of abridgement of our precious First Amendment freedoms is too great where officials have unbridled discretion over a forum's use."

The performance of a musical is protected by the First Amendment. Accordingly, the refusal of the board to permit the performance of *Hair* in the municipal theater solely because of its content constituted a prior restraint on First Amendment activity.

Although a system of prior restraint is not unconstitutional per se, it bears a heavy presumption of unconstitutionality. It is settled, moreover, that "a system of prior restraint 'avoids constitutional infirmity only if it takes place under procedural safeguards designed to obviate the dangers of a censorship system.' "

In *Freedman* v. *Maryland*, 380 U.S. 51 (1965), the Court held that these safeguards must place on the censor the burden of instituting judicial proceedings and of proving that the material in question is not protected by the First Amendment, must permit any restraint, prior to judicial review, only for a specified brief period and solely for the purpose of preserving the status quo, and must require a prompt judicial determination of the legality of the censor's restraint.

Several of the procedural safeguards required by *Freedman* were lacking in this case. The decision of the board was not subject to prompt judicial review. The promoter, not the board, had the burden of seeking judicial review and the burden of proving that its performance was protected by the First Amendment. Finally, "[d]uring the time prior to judicial determination, the restraint altered the status quo. [The promoter] was forced to forgo the initial dates planned for the engagement and to seek to schedule the performance at a later date."

## *Withrow* v. *Larkin*, 421 U.S. 35 (1975)

*Facts:* Under a Wisconsin statute, an examining board composed of practicing physicians was empowered to suspend temporarily or revoke medical licenses or institute criminal action for professional misconduct. After investigating the conduct of a physician (Dr. Larkin), the board notified him that a hearing would be held to determine whether he had engaged in certain prohibited acts that would justify temporary suspension of his license. Before the hearing, but after the board had formally found probable cause to believe that Dr. Larkin had engaged in misconduct, Larkin sued in federal district court to enjoin the board from acting further in his case.

He contended that the statutory authority given the board to investigate physicians, present charges, rule on those charges, and impose sanctions violated his procedural due process right to an independent and neutral decision maker. The district court issued a preliminary injunction against the board on the ground that the challenge to the statute's constitutionality had a high likelihood of success.

*Question:* Did the district court err in issuing the preliminary injunction?

*Decision:* Yes. Opinion by Justice White. Vote: 9–0.

*Reasons:* It is settled law that a biased decision maker in either judicial or administrative proceedings is "constitutionally unacceptable."

> In pursuit of this end, various situations have been identified in which experience teaches that the probability of actual bias on the part of the judge or decisionmaker is too high to be constitutionally tolerable. Among these cases are those in which the adjudicator has a pecuniary interest in the outcome and in which he has been the target of personal abuse or criticism from the party before him.
>
> The contention that the combination of investigative and adjudicative functions necessarily creates an unconstitutional risk of bias in administrative adjudication has a much more difficult burden of persuasion to carry. It must overcome a presumption of honesty and integrity in those serving as adjudicators; and it must convince that, under a realistic appraisal of psychological tendencies and human weakness, conferring investigative and adjudicative powers on the same individuals poses such a risk of actual bias or prejudgment that the practice must be forbidden if the guarantee of due process is to be adequately implemented.

But past Supreme Court decisions do not support the claim that agency members who participate in an investigation are ipso facto constitutionally disqualified from adjudicating. In this case, the procedures used by the board did not create an "unacceptable risk of bias." Its investigative proceedings were open to Dr. Larkin and his counsel. No showing was made that the investigation would prevent the board from rendering its decision at the contested hearing solely on the basis of the evidence presented. "The mere exposure to evidence presented in nonadversary investigative procedures is insufficient in itself to impugn the fairness of the board members at a later adversary hearing."

The board also was not automatically barred from proceeding with the contested hearing because it had issued

> formal findings of fact and conclusions of law asserting that there was probable cause to believe that [Dr. Larkin] had engaged in various acts prohibited by the Wisconsin statutes....
>
> The risk of bias or prejudgment in this sequence of functions has not been considered to be intolerably high or to raise a sufficiently great possibility that the adjudicators would be so psychologically wedded to their complaints that they would consciously or unconsciously avoid the appearance of having erred or changed position. Indeed, just as there is no logical inconsistency between a finding of probable cause and an acquittal in a criminal proceeding, there is no incompatibility between the agency filing a complaint based on probable cause and a subsequent decision, when all the evidence is in, that there has been no violation of the statute.

Accordingly, the district court erred in issuing the preliminary injunction on the ground that the combination of investigatory and adjudicatory functions, without more, violates due process. That conclusion, however, does not preclude the district court, on remand, from determining that special facts and circumstances in this case have created a sufficiently high risk of unfairness at the contested hearing to make it unconstitutional.

### *Austin* v. *New Hampshire*, 420 U.S. 656 (1975)

*Facts:* Residents of Maine who were employed in New Hampshire challenged the constitutionality of the New Hampshire Commuters Income Tax on the ground, *inter alia,* that it violated the privileges and immunity clause of the Constitution. The Commuters Income Tax imposed a tax at a rate of 4 percent on income in excess of $2,000 derived in New Hampshire by nonresidents. If, however, the nonresident's own state would impose a lesser tax had the income been earned there, the New Hampshire tax would be reduced to that amount. New Hampshire did not impose any income tax on its own residents.

*Question:* Does the challenged Commuters Income Tax violate the privileges and immunities clause?

*Decision:* Yes. Opinion by Justice Marshall. Vote: 7–1, Blackmun dissenting. Douglas did not participate.

*Reasons:* The Court reasoned that

> the Privileges and Immunities Clause . . . provides: "The citizens of each state shall be entitled to all privileges and immunities of citizens in the several states." The clause thus establishes a norm of comity without specifying the particular subjects as to which citizens of one State coming within the jurisdiction of another are guaranteed equality of treatment.

The clause was intended, however, to preclude a state from making noncitizenship or nonresidence a basis for imposing a special burden.

Earlier cases have interpreted the clause to require "substantial equality of treatment for the citizens of the taxing State and nonresident taxpayers." Accordingly, the challenged tax cannot be sustained because it falls exclusively on the incomes of nonresidents; "and it is not offset even approximately by other taxes imposed on residents alone."

The Court rejected the argument of New Hampshire that its tax should be upheld because it would be inapplicable to Maine residents if Maine repealed its credit provision for income taxes paid to another state. "[T]he constitutionality of one State's statutes affecting nonresidents [may not] depend upon the present configuration of the statutes of another State."

## *Albemarle Paper Co. v. Moody,* 422 U.S. 405 (1975)

*Facts:* Present and former employees of Albemarle Paper Co. (Albemarle) brought suit against Albemarle and their union alleging violations of Title VII of the Civil Rights Act of 1964. First, the employees alleged that the company's seniority system perpetuated the effects of past racial discrimination. Second, they claimed that Albemarle used certain preemployment tests which had a racially discriminatory effect and lacked a sufficient relation to job performance to satisfy Title VII. The employees sought injunctive relief against the existing seniority system, the use of the preemployment tests, and back pay for losses suffered under the seniority system. The back-pay remedy was requested five years after the initial complaint was filed. A federal district court held that the challenged seniority system violated Title VII but refused to award back pay. It reasoned that Albemarle had made attempts in good faith to comply with Title VII and might have been prejudiced by the delay of the employees in seeking back pay. Accordingly, it declined to exercise its authority under Title VII, 42 U.S.C. 2000e-5(g), to order back pay. The district court also found that the challenged preemployment tests were substantially related to job performance and thus complied with Title VII requirements specified in 42 U.S.C. 2000e-2(h). (In *Griggs* v. *Duke Power Co.*, 401 U.S. 424 [1971], the Court held that those provisions forbid the use of employment tests that are racially discriminatory in effect unless the employer meets "the burden of showing that any given requirement [has] . . . a manifest relation to the employment in question.")

*Questions:* (1) Did the district court use an improper standard for determining whether back pay was an appropriate remedy? (2) Did the district court err in concluding that the preemployment tests had been properly validated as measuring probable job performance?

*Decision:* Yes to both questions. Opinion by Justice Stewart. Vote: 7–1, Burger dissenting. Powell did not participate.

*Reasons:* The authority to award back pay under Title VII "was bestowed by Congress, as part of a complex legislative design directed at an historic evil of national proportions." The primary objective of Title VII

> "was to achieve equality of employment opportunities and remove barriers that have operated in the past to favor an identifiable group of white employees over other employees." Backpay has an obvious connection with this purpose. If employers faced only the prospect of an injunctive order, they would have little incentive to shun practices of dubious legality. It is the reasonably certain prospect of a backpay award that "provide[s] the spur or catalyst which causes employers and unions to self-examine and to self-evaluate their employment practices and to endeavor to eliminate, so far as possible, the last vestiges of an unfortunate and ignominious page in this country's history.". . . It is also the purpose of Title VII to make persons whole for injuries suffered on account of unlawful employment discrimination. . . .
> It follows that, given a finding of unlawful discrimination, backpay should be denied only for reasons which, if applied generally, would not frustrate the central statutory purposes of eradicating discrimination throughout the economy and

making persons whole for injuries suffered through past discrimination.

The district court thus erred in concluding that Albemarle's good faith was a sufficient reason for denying back pay. That conclusion would effectively undermine the "make whole" purpose in Title VII. It would not offend the broad purposes of Title VII, however, if back pay were denied because an unexcusable delay in requesting such relief in fact prejudiced the ability of the employer to defend the claim. Whether the five-year delay in this case justifies denial of back pay will be an issue for the district court on remand.

The procedures used to validate the preemployment tests must be measured against the Equal Employment Opportunities Commission (EEOC) guidelines.

> The EEOC Guidelines are not administrative "regulations" promulgated pursuant to formal procedures established by the Congress. But . . . they do constitute "[t]he administrative interpretation of the Act by the enforcing agency," and consequently they are "entitled to great deference.". . .
>
> The message of these Guidelines is the same as that of the *Griggs* case—that discriminatory tests are impermissible unless shown, by professionally acceptable methods, to be "predictive of or significantly correlated with important elements of work behavior which comprise or are relevant to the job or jobs for which candidates are being evaluated."

Albemarle's validation study was deficient in at least four respects: failure to show a correlation between tests and performance in all jobs; failure to use explicit criteria by which supervisors were to measure job performance; a limiting of the study to top-level job groups; and application of the study to job-experienced white workers, but not to new job applicants.

## *Cantrell* v. *Forest City Publishing Co.*, 419 U.S. 245 (1974)

*Facts:* A mother and her son brought suit against a newspaper publisher, reporter, and photographer for invasion of privacy. The theory of the plaintiffs' case was that the defendants had published a false feature story relating to the death of their husband and father which made them the objects of pity and ridicule. The story allegedly caused the plaintiffs to suffer outrage, mental distress, shame, and humiliation. The jury returned a verdict for compensatory damages after the district court instructed them that liability could be imposed only if it concluded that the false statements in the feature story had been made with knowledge of their falsity or in reckless disregard of the truth. (In *Time Inc.* v. *Hill*, 385 U.S. 374 [1967], the Court held that the First Amendment prohibited the award of compensatory damages for invasion of privacy in suits against the press based upon "false reports of matters of public interest in the absence of proof that the defendant published the report with knowledge of its falsity or in reckless disregard of the truth.") The court of appeals reversed on the ground that publication of the challenged story was protected by the First Amendment.

*Question:* Did the jury verdict for compensatory damages violate the First Amendment's protection of free speech and press?

*Decision:* No. Opinion by Justice Stewart. Vote: 8–1, Douglas dissenting.

*Reasons:* Since the district court instructed the jury under the *Time Inc.* v. *Hill* standards, "this case presents no occasion to consider whether a State may constitutionally apply a more relaxed standard of liability for a publisher or broadcaster of false statements injurious to a private individual under a false-light theory of invasion of privacy. . . ." Under the *Time* standards, there was clearly sufficient evidence to support a finding by the jury that the defendants' feature story contained knowing or reckless falsehoods. The story

> plainly implied that [the mother] had been present during [the reporter's] visit to her home and that [he] had observed her "wear[ing] the same mask of nonexpression she wore [at her husband's] funeral." These were "calculated falsehoods," and the jury was plainly justified in finding that [the reporter] had portrayed the [family] in a false light through knowing or reckless untruth.

### Elections and Voting Rights

The Court ruled on a variety of issues having to do with election law and voting rights: reapportionment, selection of delegates to national party conventions, illegal campaign contributions, municipal bond elections, and the Voting Rights Act.

In holding unconstitutional a reapportionment plan devised by a district court, the Supreme Court stated that such plans must avoid using multimember districts absent compelling reasons. In addition, the Court decided that court-ordered reapportionment plans must be drawn with less population variance between districts than is permissible with legislatively devised plans.[22]

In a decision of great significance for both Republican and Democratic national parties, the Court concluded in *Cousins* v. *Wigoda,* 419 U.S. 477, that the states lack any authority to control the method by which delegates are selected to a national party convention to nominate presidential and vice-presidential candidates. That conclusion has clear implications for the Democratic and Republican parties in the selection of their presidential candidates. For example, if the party leadership in a national committee supports a candidate likely to obtain more delegate support through party conventions as opposed to primaries, then under *Cousins* the committee may ignore state laws calling for the selection of delegates through primaries and instead use the convention method of selection.

In *Hill* v. *Stone*, 421 U.S. 289, the Court adhered to its earlier decisions which established the general rule that the franchise in municipal bond elections may not be constitutionally limited to property taxpayers.[23]

Because of recent disclosures that numerous corporations have made sizeable illegal political campaign expenditures in past years, the case of *Cort* v. *Ash*, 422 U.S. 66, became important. At issue was whether a federal criminal statute prohibiting such contributions also granted stockholders a right to recover damages against the corporate directors who made the illegal expenditures. The Court concluded that the stockholders lacked any such rights under the statute.

In *City of Richmond* v. *United States*, 422 U.S. 358, the Court decided two significant questions under the Voting Rights Act. First, it concluded that city annexations which reduce the percentage of black voters in the city are proper so long as the post-annexation electoral scheme fairly reflects the voting strength of the black community. Second, it ruled that annexations which were initially tainted by a racially discriminatory motive could be sustained if justified by current legitimate objective reasons such as economic or administrative advantages.

---

[22] A legislatively enacted apportionment plan for a state legislative body may constitutionally provide for interdistrict population variances of up to 10 percent, White v. Regester, 412 U.S. 755 (1973), and up to at least 16 percent if justified by special state interests, Mahan v. Howell, 410 U.S. 315 (1973). Reapportionment plans for congressional districts must satisfy more rigorous standards of population equality. See White v. Weiser, 412 U.S. 783 (1973).

[23] See Kramer v. Union Free School District No. 15, 395 U.S. 621 (1969); Cipriano v. City of Houma, 395 U.S. 701 (1969); Phoenix v. Kolodziejski, 399 U.S. 204 (1970).

## *Cousins* v. *Wigoda*, 419 U.S. 477 (1975)

*Facts:* In the March 1972 Illinois primary election, the Democratic voters of Chicago elected fifty-nine delegates (Wigoda delegates) to the 1972 Democratic National Convention. So-called Cousins delegates successfully challenged the seating of the Wigoda delegates before the credentials committee of the national Democratic party on the ground that the Wigoda delegates were selected under procedures which violated party guidelines. After the credentials committee decided that the Cousins delegates should be seated, the Wigoda delegates obtained an injunction from an Illinois state court barring the Cousins group from acting as delegates at the convention. In defiance of the injunction, the Cousins delegates took their seats and participated fully throughout the convention. The injunction was later affirmed by an Illinois appellate court on the ground that state law determined the right to sit as a delegate representing Illinois at the national nominating convention. It rejected the contention of the Cousins delegates that the injunction violated their right, and the right of the national Democratic party, to freedom of political activity and association guaranteed them under the First and Fourteenth amendments.

*Question:* Was the injunction issued by the state court unconstitutional?

*Decision:* Yes. Opinion by Justice Brennan. Vote: 8–1, Powell dissenting.

*Reasons:* "The National Democratic Party and its adherents enjoy a constitutionally protected right of political association." Any interference with these rights can be justified only by a compelling state interest. It is argued that the challenged injunction was justified by the "interest [of Illinois] in protecting the integrity of its electoral processes and the right of its citizens under the state and federal constitutions to effective suffrage." But these arguments overlook the fact that the suffrage in this case was exercised to elect delegates to a national party convention to nominate presidential and vice-presidential candidates. States have no constitutionally mandated role in this process.

> If the qualifications and eligibility of delegates to National Political Party Conventions were left to state law ". . . each of the 50 states could establish the qualifications of its delegates to the various party conventions without regard to

party policy, an obviously intolerable result.". . . Such a regime could seriously undercut or indeed destroy the effectiveness of the National Party Convention as a concerted enterprise engaged in the vital process of choosing Presidential and Vice-Presidential candidates—a process which usually involves coalitions cutting across state lines. The Convention serves the pervasive national interest in the selection of candidates for national office, and this national interest is greater than any interest of an individual State. . . .

Thus, Illinois' interest in protecting the integrity of its electoral process cannot be deemed compelling in the context of the selection of delegates to the National Party Convention.

## *Chapman* v. *Meier*, 420 U.S. 1 (1975)

*Facts:* Following protracted state and federal litigation, a three-judge federal district court approved a 1965 reapportionment plan for the North Dakota Legislative Assembly which included five multimember senatorial districts. In 1971, before another three-judge federal court, a suit challenged the constitutionality of the 1965 reapportionment plan, alleging that substantial shifts in population had occurred since 1965 and that the plan was thus in violation of the one-man, one-vote rule mandated by the equal protection clause. The plaintiffs requested that reapportionment be ordered on the basis of the 1970 census and that it provide for single-member districts. Concluding that the 1965 plan failed to meet constitutional standards, the court ordered another plan containing five multimember senatorial districts and a 20 percent population variance between the largest and smallest senatorial districts. The plaintiffs appealed, contending that the use of multimember senatorial districts was improper and that the 20 percent population variance between senatorial districts was unconstitutional.

*Question:* Is the court-ordered reapportionment plan defective as contended by the plaintiffs?

*Decision:* Yes. Opinion by Justice Blackmun. Vote: 9–0.

*Reasons:* Although multimember districts in apportionment plans adopted by states for their legislatures are not unconstitutional per se, three reasons militate against their use.

First, as the number of legislative seats within the district increases, the difficulty for the voter in making intelligent choices among candidates also increases. . . . Ballots tend to become unwieldy, confusing, and too lengthy to allow thoughtful consideration. Second, when candidates are elected at-large, residents of particular areas within the district may feel that they have no representative specially responsible to them. Third, it is possible that bloc voting by delegates from a multimember district may result in undue representation of residents of these districts relative to voters in single-member districts.

Accordingly, the Court has adopted a rule in the exercise of its supervisory power over lower federal courts that court-imposed apportionment plans should avoid multimember districts absent compelling reasons justifying their use. In this case, the district court failed to articulate any strong reasons for using multimember districts; thus, their use was improper.

The challenged 20 percent population variance was unconstitutional because the district court failed to elucidate any significant state policy which would necessitate such a departure from approximate population equality among districts. In *White* v. *Regester,* 412 U.S. 755 (1973), the Court indicated that any population variance exceeding 10 percent would violate the general requirement established in *Reynolds* v. *Sims,* 377 U.S. 533 (1964), that both houses of a state legislature be apportioned so that districts are as nearly of equal population as practicable, unless the variance was "based on legitimate considerations incident to the effectuation of a rational state policy."

The district court advanced three reasons to justify its variance: (1) the absence of electorally victimized minorities in North Dakota; (2) its sparse population; and (3) adherence to natural geographic boundaries and existing political subdivisions. The first two reasons cannot justify a departure from the goal of population equality in any circumstances. The third was not shown to require a 20 percent variance. Indeed, the record demonstrated that the policy of respecting geographical boundaries and maintaining township lines could be satisfied with a significantly lower population variance.

The challenged court-ordered reapportionment plan thus

fails to meet the standards established for evaluating variances in plans formulated by state legislatures or other state bodies. . . . A court-ordered plan, however, must be held to higher standards than a State's own plan. With a court plan, any deviation from approximate population equality must be supported by enunciation of historically significant state policy or unique features.

## *Hill* v. *Stone*, 421 U.S. 289 (1975)

*Facts:* Provisions in the Texas constitution restrict the franchise in municipal bond elections to otherwise qualified voters who pay real or personal property taxes. Any person may voluntarily list property for taxation, however, no matter how small in value, and thereby qualify for the franchise. The provisions restricting the franchise were challenged as unconstitutional in connection with a city election to authorize bonds for the purpose of constructing a library. It was contended that to disfranchise persons for failure to pay property taxes violated the equal protection clause of the Fourteenth Amendment.

*Question:* Are the challenged provisions restricting the franchise to property taxpayers unconstitutional?

*Decision:* Yes. Opinion by Justice Marshall. Vote: 5–3, Burger, Stewart, and Rehnquist dissenting. Douglas did not participate.

*Reasons: Kramer* v. *Union Free School District,* 395 U.S. 621 (1969), *Cipriano* v. *City of Houma,* 395 U.S. 701 (1969), and *City of Phoenix* v. *Kolodziejski,* 399 U.S. 204 (1970), established the basic principle "that as long as the election in question is not one of special interest, any classification restricting the franchise on grounds other than residence, age, and citizenship cannot stand unless the district or State can demonstrate that the classification serves a compelling state interest." The bond election at issue in this case was not one of special interest, even though the debt service will be paid entirely out of property taxes. Two reasons underlie this conclusion. First, construction of a library is of general interest to the community. Second, a substantial portion of taxes levied against commercial property is treated as a business expense. These taxes are reflected in the prices of goods and services purchased by nonproperty owners and property owners alike. Thus, the ultimate burden of property taxes is not assumed solely by those directly taxed.

It is argued that the challenged restriction serves the state's compelling interest in encouraging prospective voters to list all their property voluntarily for taxation. That contention is unpersuasive. Those listing property

> solely to earn the right to vote in bond elections may well [list] property of minimal value, in order to qualify for voting without imposing upon themselves a substantial tax liability. The [voluntary listing] requirement thus seems unlikely to have any significant impact on the asserted state policy of encouraging each person to [list] all of his property.

## *Cort* v. *Ash,* 422 U.S. 66 (1975)

*Facts:* A stockholder of Bethlehem Steel Corporation brought suit for damages against the chairman of its board of directors alleging unlawful expenditure by the chairman of corporate funds under 18 U.S.C. 610, in opposition to a candidate, Senator McGovern, in the 1972 presidential election. It is a crime under section 610 for a corporation to make expenditures in connection with any federal election. A federal district court dismissed the claim for damages and injunctive relief on the ground that section 610 did not afford a private right of action against corporate directors.

*Question:* Is a private right of action for damages against corporate directors implied in favor of a stockholder under section 610?

*Decision:* No. Opinion by Justice Brennan. Vote: 9–0.

*Reasons:* The unanimous opinion stated that

> in determining whether a private remedy is implicit in a statute not expressly providing one, several factors are relevant. First, is the plaintiff "one of the class for whose *especial* benefit the statute was enacted," . . . that is, does the statute create a federal right in favor of the plaintiff? Second, is there any indication of legislative intent, explicit or implicit, either to create such a remedy or to deny one? . . . Third, is it consistent with the underlying purposes of the legislative scheme to imply such a remedy for the plaintiff? . . . And finally, is the cause of action one traditionally relegated to state law, in an area basically the concern of the States, so that it would be inappropriate to infer a cause of action based solely on federal law? (Emphasis in original.)

Consideration of these factors militates against implying a private right of action. The main purpose of section 610 was to eliminate the influence over elections which corporations exercised through financial contributions. Protecting stockholders from use of their invested funds for political purposes was, at best, a secondary concern. In addition, "there is no indication whatever in the legislative history of section 610 which suggests a congressional intention to vest in corporate shareholders a federal right to damages for violation of section 610." Moreover, recovery of damages "would not cure the influence which the use of corporate funds in the first instance may have had on a federal election." Finally, improper use of corporate funds is a traditional concern of state law.

It is unnecessary to decide whether a private cause of action for injunctive relief is available under section 610. Under the Federal

Election Campaign Act Amendments of 1974, a private complainant must first seek such relief from the Federal Election Commission. The commission has authority to request the attorney general to obtain an injunction forbidding violations of section 610. Relief through the Federal Election Commission was not pursued in this case.

## *City of Richmond* v. *United States,* 422 U.S. 358 (1975)

*Facts:* In 1969, the city of Richmond, Virginia, annexed adjacent land in predominantly white Chesterfield County. The annexation reduced the proportion of Negroes in Richmond from 52 percent to 42 percent. The pre-annexation nine-member city council was elected at large. Following the decision in *Perkins* v. *Matthews,* 400 U.S. 379 (1971), holding that section 5 of the Voting Rights Act covers annexations, Richmond brought suit in the federal district court for the District of Columbia seeking a declaration that its annexation had neither the purpose nor the effect of abridging the right to vote on account of race. (Under section 5, certain states or political subdivisions generally may not change any voting law without the prior approval of either the attorney general or the federal district court for the District of Columbia. Approval is proper only if the state or political subdivision sustains the burden of proving that the change will not have a racially discriminatory purpose or effect.) Richmond's post-annexation city council plan would create nine single-member wards: four with substantial black majorities, four with substantial white majorities, and one 59 percent white and 41 percent black. The district court ruled that the annexation had a racially discriminatory purpose and effect. It found that its purpose was to dilute black voting power and lacked any legitimate goal. It also concluded that the ward voting system had the effect of discriminating against Negro voters because the wards could have been drawn in a fashion to improve the chance that Negroes would control five of the council seats.

*Question:* Did the annexation have an impermissible racially discriminatory purpose or effect?

*Decision:* It had no racially discriminatory effect, but further proceedings are needed to determine whether its purpose was racially tainted. Opinion by Justice White. Vote: 5–3, Brennan, Douglas, and Marshall dissenting. Powell did not participate.

*Reasons:* To conclude that the single-member ward plan had a racially discriminatory effect because Negroes would constitute a lesser proportion of the population after the annexation than before and, given racial bloc voting, would have fewer seats on the city council [would be improper]. If a city having a ward system for the election of a nine-man council annexes a largely white area, the wards are fairly redrawn, and as a result Negroes have only two rather than the four seats they had before, these facts alone do not demonstrate that the annexation has the effect of denying or abridging the right to vote. As long as the ward system fairly reflects the strength of the Negro community as it exists after the annexation, we cannot hold, without more specific legislative directions, that such an annexation is nevertheless barred by section 5. . . . To hold otherwise would be either to forbid all such annexations or to require, as the price for approval of the annexation, that the black community be assigned the same proportion of council seats as before, hence perhaps permanently over-representing them and underrepresenting other elements in the community, including the nonblack citizens in the annexed area. We are unwilling to hold that Congress intended either consequence in enacting section 5.

Here the proposed ward plan did not undervalue the black voting strength in the post-annexation community and thus had no racially discriminatory effect for purposes of section 5.

Nevertheless, if the annexation was motivated by a racially discriminatory purpose, it is barred by that section. Although clearly infected by this impermissible purpose in 1969, the annexation must be sustained if objective legitimate reasons such as economic or administrative advantages are now demonstrable to support it. Since the record may be incomplete on this issue, further proceedings are desirable.

## Federal Courts and Procedure

Many Supreme Court decisions in the 1970s seem part of a trend toward returning to the states a greater responsibility for the resolution of political, economic, and social problems. General and special revenue-sharing legislation has been a response, at least in part, to claims that the states can allocate money to the treatment of community problems more effectively than can the Congress.[24] Beginning

---

[24] See Housing and Community Development Act of 1974, 88 Stat. 633 (1974); Education Amendments of 1974, 88 Stat. 484 (1974); Comprehensive Employment and Training Act of 1973, 87 Stat. 839 (1973); State and Local Fiscal Assistance Act of 1972, 86 Stat. 919 (1972).

with its 1971 decision in *Younger* v. *Harris,* 401 U.S. 37 (1971), the Supreme Court has established a general doctrine of federal abstention from interference in ongoing state criminal proceedings.[25] This doctrine reflects a desire to permit state courts an opportunity to resolve constitutional disputes in the first instance.

This term the Court expanded the application of the *Younger* doctrine. It held that federal courts must abstain from interference in state civil proceedings and military courts-martial absent the extraordinary circumstances defined in *Younger.* The Court also ruled that the abstention doctrine of *Younger* applied to federal suits filed before the commencement of a state prosecution if the state prosecution began before "proceedings of substance" occurred in the federal court.[26]

In reversing a court of appeals decision in *Kugler* v. *Helfant,* 421 U.S. 117, the Court reiterated that the occasions justifying a departure from *Younger,* in light of special circumstances, are few.

The problem of federal interference in state criminal proceedings was also raised under a civil rights removal statute enacted after the Civil War. Generally speaking, that statute permits a state defendant to remove his trial to a federal court if he cannot enforce in the state court "a right under any law providing for equal civil rights." The Court interpreted the statute narrowly in concluding that it did not protect Negroes prosecuted for picketing and urging a boycott of businesses because of their alleged racial discrimination in employment.

The increasing caseload of the Supreme Court has become a focus of national attention. In 1971, the chief justice appointed a group of legal experts, headed by Professor Paul A. Freund of the Harvard Law School, to study the caseload problem and to make recommendations. One of the group's recommendations was the elimination by statute of three-judge district courts and mandatory direct review of their decisions by the Supreme Court.[27] Approximately 22 percent of all cases argued orally before the Supreme Court involve direct review of three-judge court decisions pursuant to 28

---

[25] There the Court held that federal injunctions sought after the commencement of state criminal proceedings could be issued only under extraordinary circumstances, in which the danger that the state proceedings would cause irreparable loss is both great and immediate.

[26] See Huffman v. Pursue, Ltd., 420 U.S. 592 (1975); Schlesinger v. Councilman, 420 U.S. 739 (1975); Hicks v. Miranda, 422 U.S. 332 (1975).

[27] See *Report of the Study Group on the Caseload of the Supreme Court* (Washington, D.C.: Federal Judicial Center, 1972), p. 29. See Chapter 1, note 24. The Court has discretion whether or not to review most other cases.

U.S.C. 1253.[28] That statute has been sharply criticized by Chief Justice Burger because it limits the Supreme Court's control over its docket. Justices Brennan, Marshall, Blackmun, and Powell have also indicated support for repeal of section 1253.[29]

Despite these weighty attacks on section 1253, Congress did not complete action on this repeal proposal until August 1976.[30] Perhaps motivated by frustration, the Court itself during the 1974–75 term provided some relief from the mandatory review provisions of that statute. In a strained interpretation overruling numerous past decisions, the Court held that section 1253 authorized direct review from a three-judge court decision denying injunctive relief only if the decision resolves the merits of the constitutional claims raised. That is, decisions denying injunctive relief for lack of justiciability or subject matter jurisdiction or because abstention is appropriate will not be directly reviewed by the Supreme Court. The Court acknowledged that its interpretation departed from the plain language of section 1253 authorizing without qualification direct review of three-judge court decisions "denying . . . an . . . injunction in any civil action."

Federal district courts and courts of appeals also are burdened by expanding caseloads. During fiscal year 1975, 160,602 suits were filed in district courts, an increase of 12 percent over the number filed the previous year. During that same period, there were 16,658 filings in the courts of appeals, an increase of 1.4 percent over the number filed the preceding year. No additional appellate judgeships have been authorized since 1968, when the number reached 97. Since 1966, the number of appeals filed per judgeship has increased from 82 to 172.[31] During the same period, the number of cases filed per district judgeship, calculated on a weighted basis giving a disproportionately large count to complex and lengthy cases, has risen from 225 to 400.[32] Chief Justice Burger has severely criticized Congress

---

[28] Most three-judge courts are required when suits are brought seeking to enjoin enforcement of a state or federal statute on constitutional grounds. See 28 U.S.C. 2281, 2282.

[29] See Commission on Revision of the Federal Court Appellate System, *Structure and Internal Procedures: Recommendations for Change* (Washington, D.C.: U.S. Government Printing Office, June 1975). In stark contrast to these views, Justice Douglas wrote in Warth v. Seldin, 422 U.S. 490 (1975): "[No] Justice of this [Supreme] Court need work more than four days a week to carry his burden. I have found it a comfortable burden carried even in my months of hospitalization."

[30] See Chapter 1, note 24.

[31] See *1975 Annual Report of the Director, Administrative Office of the United States Courts*, p. XI-10 to XI-16.

[32] See ibid., p. XI-124.

for failing to create additional federal judgeships while it continues to enact legislation increasing the burdens of federal courts.[33]

Two decisions of the Court will operate to discourage federal lawsuits and thereby tend to relieve the caseload of the federal judiciary. In ruling that attorneys' fees should not be awarded to the environmental groups that had successfully sued to enjoin the construction of the trans-Alaskan oil pipeline, the Court concluded that federal courts lack the inherent authority to award such fees in suits brought to vindicate important public interests. Only federal legislation, the Court stated, can provide such authority. This decision may increase the difficulty of obtaining lawyers to represent so-called public-interest groups.

Utilizing the constitutional requirement of "standing," the Court erected a barrier to gaining access to federal courts in *Warth* v. *Seldin,* 422 U.S. 490. Standing is an element of the constitutional limitation on federal judicial power to decide "cases" or "controversies" in Article III, section 2. To obtain standing, a plaintiff must allege some concrete injury to himself that has been substantially caused by the defendant. In a sharply divided 5–4 decision, the Court applied the standing doctrine to dismiss three categories of plaintiffs seeking to challenge the constitutionality of suburban zoning practices which allegedly precluded the building of low- and moderate-income housing. The basis of the Court's opinion was that no plaintiff alleged that he would immediately profit if the claimed unconstitutional zoning practices were corrected. It is unclear whether *Warth* v. *Seldin* will merely require more artful pleading by plaintiffs or will in fact operate to eliminate standing for a significant group of potential plaintiffs.

Mr. Justice Powell wrote in *Warth* that citizens dissatisfied with restrictive suburban zoning laws "need not overlook the availability of the normal democratic process," indicating that the courts should not always be sought as the first avenue of redress for perceived grievances. That statement reflects an attitude by the Burger Court

---

[33] In his annual state of the judiciary report to the American Bar Association on February 15, 1975, the chief justice suggested that a Congress controlled by the Democratic party was refusing for partisan reasons to create judgeships that would be filled by a Republican President. Referring to pending legislation that would create additional circuit and district judgeships, he stated:

"In the near crisis situation that confronts us [in the federal judiciary], I put to you whether any political considerations related to the impending presidential election are tolerable."

The Senate has passed legislation that would create seven additional circuit judgeships, S. 286, 94th Congress, 1st sess. (1975), and 45 additional district judgeships, S. 287, 94th Congress, 2nd sess. (1976).

that an "undemocratically" selected federal judiciary is not the constitutionally appropriate branch for resolving all disputes that can be fashioned into a legal posture.[34]

## *Hicks* v. *Miranda*, 422 U.S. 332 (1975)

*Facts:* In November 1973, four copies of an allegedly obscene film (*Deep Throat*) were seized pursuant to a search warrant, and two employees of a theater which had shown that film were charged with violating California's obscenity statute. The theater owner filed suit in federal district court seeking on constitutional grounds to enjoin enforcement of the state obscenity statutes and to recover all copies of the film. In January 1974, the theater owner was added as a criminal defendant in the obscenity prosecution against his two employees. A three-judge federal district court was convened to hear the owner's claims for injunctive relief under 28 U.S.C. 2281. (That section requires three-judge federal district courts to hear suits seeking to enjoin the enforcement of a state statute on substantial constitutional grounds.) In sustaining the owner's claims, the federal district court rejected the contention of state officials that the suit should be dismissed under principles of federalism announced in *Younger* v. *Harris*, 401 U.S. 66 (1971). The district court also disregarded a decision by the United States Supeme Court dismissing "for want of a substantial federal question" an appeal from a state court decision upholding the constitutionality of California's obscenity statute in *Miller* v. *California*, 418 U.S. 915 (1974), memorandum decision (known as *Miller II*). The decision of the federal district court was directly appealed to the Supreme Court under 28 U.S.C. 1253.

*Question:* (1) Was a direct appeal to the Supreme Court authorized under section 1253? (2) Should the federal district court have dismissed the owner's suit under the principles of federalism established in *Younger* v. *Harris*?

*Decision:* Yes to both questions. Opinion by Justice White. Vote: 5–4, Stewart, Douglas, Brennan, and Marshall dissenting.

*Reasons:* Section 1253 authorizes a direct appeal to the Supreme Court from suits required to be heard by three-judge federal district

---

[34] See U.S. v. Richardson, 418 U.S. 166 (1974); Schlesinger v. Reservists Committee to Stop the War, 418 U.S. 208 (1974).

courts. Under 28 U.S.C. 2281, however, three-judge district courts are not required to hear "insubstantial" constitutional claims. In determining the substantiality of the constitutional challenge to the obscenity statute, the three-judge federal district court erred in disregarding *Miller II*. A dismissal for want of a substantial federal question is a decision on the merits. It represents a conclusion that the constitutional issue raised is insubstantial, and such a conclusion is binding on lower federal courts. Nevertheless, direct appeal under section 1253 was still proper because a three-judge court was required to hear the claim challenging the constitutionality of the state search warrant statute.

The district court erred in refusing to dismiss the constitutional claims under *Younger* v. *Harris*. There the Court held that federal courts should abstain from interference in pending state criminal proceedings unless the state charges were brought in bad faith or other great and immediate harm would result from permitting the state prosecution to continue. That rule "is designed to 'permit state courts to try state cases free from interference by federal courts,' particularly where the party to the federal case may fully litigate his claim before the state court." Although *Younger* v. *Harris* applied only to federal suits filed when state criminal proceedings were pending,

> we now hold that where state criminal proceedings are begun against the federal plaintiffs after the federal complaint is filed but before any proceedings of substance on the merits have taken place in the federal court, the principles of *Younger* v. *Harris* should apply in full force. Here, [the theater owner was] charged on January 15, prior to answering the federal case and prior to any proceedings whatsoever before the three-judge court. Unless we are to trivialize the principles of *Younger* v. *Harris*, the federal complaint should have been dismissed on the State's motion absent satisfactory proof of those extraordinary circumstances calling into play one of the limited exceptions to the rule of *Younger* v. *Harris* and related cases.

The district court erred in concluding that the state prosecution was brought in bad faith so as to justify a departure from the *Younger* v. *Harris* rule. That conclusion rested mainly upon the belief that the state courts had erred in upholding the constitutionality of the challenged search warrant and obscenity statutes. A district court may not infer official bad faith merely because it disagrees with decisions of a state court.

## *Huffman v. Pursue, Ltd.*, 420 U.S. 592 (1975)

*Facts:* Under Ohio's public nuisance statute, certain public officials instituted proceedings in state court to order a theater closed for one year and the sale of personal property used in its operation on the ground that it had been used to exhibit obscene films. When the requested relief was granted, the defendant, instead of appealing the judgment within the Ohio court system, filed suit in federal district court under 42 U.S.C. 1983, alleging the unconstitutionality of the nuisance statute. The district court concluded that the statute constituted an unconstitutional prior restraint on First Amendment rights insofar as it temporarily or permanently prevented the showing of films which had not been adjudged obscene in prior adversary hearings. Accordingly, the court permanently enjoined the execution of that portion of the state court's judgment that prohibited exhibition of films which had not been adjudged obscene. The Ohio public officials appealed on the ground, *inter alia*, that the federal district court should have abstained from deciding the case in deference to the principles of federalism enunciated in *Younger v. Harris*, 401 U.S. 37 (1971).

*Question:* Did the federal district court improperly intervene in the state civil proceeding contrary to the decision in *Younger v. Harris?*

*Decision:* Yes. Opinion by Justice Rehnquist. Vote: 6–3, Brennan, Douglas, and Marshall dissenting.

*Reasons: Younger* held that federal injunctions against state criminal proceedings could be issued only under extraordinary circumstances where the danger that the state proceedings will cause irreparable loss is both great and immediate. *Younger* indicated that such extraordinary circumstances could exist if the prosecution was for the purpose of harassment or pursuant to a patently and flagrantly unconstitutional statute. The cost and inconvenience of defending against a state prosecution in good faith, however, was not the type of injury that could justify federal interference.

The reasoning behind *Younger* was that under principles of federalism, states should ordinarily be permitted to perform their separate functions and be allowed an opportunity to vindicate federal rights without undue interference from the national government. *Younger* also rested upon the traditional reluctance of courts of equity to interfere with criminal prosecutions.

The state civil proceeding under the nuisance statute is sufficiently similar to a criminal prosecution to invoke the principles established in *Younger*.

> [T]he proceeding is both in aid of and closely related to criminal statutes which prohibit the dissemination of obscene materials. Thus, an offense to the State's interest in the nuisance litigation is likely to be every bit as great as it would be were this a criminal proceeding. . . . Similarly, while in this case the District Court's injunction has not directly disrupted Ohio's criminal justice system, it has disrupted that State's efforts to protect the very interests which underlie its criminal laws and to obtain compliance with precisely the standards which are embodied in its criminal laws.

The Court rejected the contention that *Younger* should apply only while a state proceeding is pending and not after the proceeding has ended, when only state appellate remedies are available. It reasoned that federal intervention prior to completion of state appellate proceedings would produce the evils at which *Younger* is directed: The disruption of a state's efforts to protect interests which it deems important and the deprivation of a state judicial system of the opportunity to determine constitutional claims. Accordingly, the Court held "*Younger* standards must be met to justify federal intervention in a state judicial proceeding as to which a losing litigant has not exhausted his state appellate remedies."

The case was remanded to the federal district court with directions to consider whether its intervention was justified by one of the narrow exceptions announced in *Younger*.

### *Kugler* v. *Helfant*, 421 U.S. 117 (1975)

*Facts:* Under indictment by a state grand jury for obstruction of justice and perjury, a New Jersey municipal judge brought suit in federal district court to enjoin his prosecution. He alleged that a state prosecutor and members of the New Jersey Supreme Court had unlawfully coerced his testimony before the state grand jury which led to the indictment and that the significant role played by members of the New Jersey Supreme Court in coercing his testimony made it impossible for him to receive a fair trial in the state court system. The district court dismissed the suit on the ground that *Younger* v. *Harris*, 401 U.S. 37 (1971), precluded federal intervention in the state criminal proceeding. Reversing and remanding, a court of appeals held that the district court should determine whether the allegedly coerced testimony before the grand jury should be admitted into evidence at the state trial.

*Question:* Did *Younger* v. *Harris* preclude this type of federal interference in the state criminal proceeding?

*Decision:* Yes. Opinion by Justice Stewart. Vote: 7–0. Douglas and Brennan did not participate.

*Reasons: Younger* v. *Harris* held "that in the absence of exceptional circumstances creating a threat of irreparable injury 'both great and immediate,' a federal court must not intervene by way of either injunction or declaratory judgment in a pending state criminal prosecution." *Younger* indicated that extraordinary circumstances exist if the prosecution is for purposes of harassment or it is pursuant to a flagrantly unconstitutional statute. Although these examples were not intended to be exhaustive, other circumstances are "extraordinary" only if they create a compelling need for immediate federal equitable relief. No such circumstances existed here.

New Jersey laws permit a defendant to disqualify a particular judge from participating in his case. In addition, appellate judges must disqualify themselves whenever there is any reason " 'which might preclude a fair and unbiased hearing and judgment, *or which might reasonably lead counsel or the parties to believe so.*' . . . Thus, the New Jersey judicial system provides procedural safeguards to guarantee that [the defendant judge] will not be denied due process of law in the state trial or appellate process." (Emphasis in original.) Accordingly, his claim that federal intervention is warranted because "he cannot receive a fair hearing in the state court system is without foundation."

The court of appeals erred in ordering the district court to determine whether the judge's testimony before the grand jury should be admitted in evidence at the state trial. *Perez* v. *Ledesma,* 401 U.S. 82 (1971), and *Stefanelli* v. *Minard,* 342 U.S. 117 (1951), established the principle that "the admissibility of evidence in state criminal prosecutions [is] ordinarily [a] matter to be resolved by state tribunals, subject, of course, to review by certiorari or appeal in this Court or, in a proper case, on federal habeas corpus." No extraordinary circumstances existed here which justified departing from that principle.

## *Schlesinger* v. *Councilman,* 420 U.S. 738 (1975)

*Facts:* Court-martial charges were preferred against an army captain on active duty for allegedly possessing and selling marijuana off post and not in uniform. The captain successfully obtained a federal district court injunction preventing the military authorities from proceeding with the court-martial on the ground that his alleged offenses were not "service-connected" and thus outside the jurisdiction of the court-martial. (In *O'Callahan* v. *Parker*, 395 U.S 258 [1969], the Court held that the jurisdiction of the court-martial could constitutionally reach only offenses which were "service-connected.")

*Question:* Was the federal district court's injunction proper?

*Decision:* No. Opinion by Justice Powell. Vote: 6–3, Douglas, Brennan, and Marshall dissenting.

*Reasons:* The Court first rejected the contention that the federal district court lacked jurisdiction to entertain the suit by virtue of Article 76 of the Uniform Code of Military Justice (UCMJ). That article provides in pertinent part that "the proceedings, findings, and sentences of courts-martial as approved, reviewed, or affirmed as required by this chapter . . . are final and conclusive" and "all action taken pursuant to those proceedings [is] binding upon all . . . courts of the United States." Both the legislative history of this article and the decision of the Court in *Gusik* v. *Schilder*, 340 U.S. 128 (1950), make clear that it was intended to bar review only of court-martial actions taken within the scope of its jurisdiction. Because the army captain challenged the jurisdiction of the court-martial, review by a federal district court was not barred.

Nevertheless, there remains the issue of whether the district court properly exercised its equity powers in enjoining the court-martial proceedings. General principles of equity jurisprudence forbid interference with criminal proceedings absent proof of irreparable harm which would be greater than that incident to any criminal prosecution brought in good faith. No such irreparable harm was shown in this case.

Moreover, in enacting the UCMJ,

> Congress attempted to balance . . . military necessities against the equally significant interest of ensuring fairness to servicemen charged with military offenses, and to formulate a mechanism by which these often competing interests can be adjusted. As a result, Congress created an integrated system of military courts and review procedures, a critical element of which is the Court of Military Appeals consisting of civilian judges "completely removed from military influence or persuasion," who would gain over time thorough familiarity with military problems.

Implicit in the military court system is congressional confidence in its ability to vindicate a serviceman's constitutional rights and to provide expertise in the determination of military needs. Accordingly, "when a serviceman charged with crimes by military authorities can show no harm other than that attendant to resolution of his case in the military court system, the federal district courts must refrain from intervention, by way of injunction or otherwise."

## *MTM, Inc.* v. *Baxley*, 420 U.S. 799 (1975)

*Facts:* A state court temporarily enjoined the operation of a movie theater on the ground that it constituted a nuisance because it had violated local obscenity laws. A three-judge federal district court denied the request of the movie theater to enjoin the enforcement of the temporary injunction and declare the state nuisance law unconstitutional. It reasoned that federal intervention in the state proceedings would be improper under *Younger* v. *Harris*, 401 U.S. 37 (1971), and thus dismissed the complaint without prejudice. (In *Younger* the Court held that principles of equity forbid federal courts from interfering with state criminal proceedings brought in good faith and not for purposes of harassment.) The movie theater sought Supreme Court review of the dismissal under 28 U.S.C. 1253, which authorizes an "appeal to the Supreme Court from an order . . . denying . . . an . . . injunction in any civil action . . . required . . . to be heard and determined by a district court of three judges."

*Question:* Was the three-judge federal district court decision reviewable by the Supreme Court under section 1253?

*Decision:* No. Per curiam opinion. Vote: 8–1, Douglas dissenting.

*Reasons:* In *Gonzalez* v. *Automatic Employees Credit Union*, 419 U.S. 90 (1974), the Court held that section 1253 did not authorize a direct appeal to the Supreme Court from the order of a three-judge court which dismissed a complaint because of an absence of standing, without reaching the constitutional claims presented. The Court justified its interpretation largely on the ground that the federal policy underlying section 1253 is to prevent a single judge from enjoining the operation of state or federal statutes and that this purpose would not be undermined by refusing to entertain appeals from decisions *denying* injunctive relief based upon issues short of the merits—such as justiciability, subject matter jurisdiction, equitable jurisdiction, and abstention.

> A broad construction of the statute, on the other hand, would be at odds with the historic congressional policy of minimizing the mandatory docket of this Court in the interest of sound judicial administration. . . . [Accordingly], a direct appeal will lie to this Court under section 1253 from the order of a three-judge federal court denying interlocutory or permanent injunctive relief only where such order rests upon resolution of the merits of the constitutional claim presented below.

### *Gonzalez* v. *Automatic Employees Credit Union,* 419 U.S. 90 (1974)

*Facts:* A three-judge federal district court dismissed a class action attacking the constitutionality of Illinois automobile repossession and resale statutes on the ground that the plaintiff lacked standing to maintain the suit. The plaintiff, Gonzalez, appealed directly to the Supreme Court under 28 U.S.C. 1253. That section provides, in relevant part, that "any party may appeal to the Supreme Court from an order . . . denying . . . an . . . injunction in any civil action . . . required . . . to be heard and determined by a district court of three judges." Gonzalez argued that the dismissal, in effect, denied him the requested injunctive relief and that the suit was required to be heard by a three-judge court under 28 U.S.C. 2281. (Section 2281 requires a three-judge federal court to hear a suit seeking to enjoin the operation of a state statute on the ground of its unconstitutionality.)

*Question:* Was the order of the three-judge court dismissing the complaint for lack of standing directly appealable to the Supreme Court under 28 U.S.C. 1253?

*Decision:* No. Opinion by Justice Stewart. Vote: 9–0.

*Reasons:* Although "the Court has on several occasions entertained direct appeals from three-judge court orders denying injunctions on grounds short of the merits . . . it is also a fact that in the area of statutory three-judge court law the doctrine of stare decisis has historically been accorded considerably less than its usual weight." Accordingly, it is appropriate to review the purpose of section 1253 to determine whether it should be construed to authorize an appeal in this case.

"Congress established the three-judge court apparatus for one reason: to save state and federal statutes from improvident doom, on constitutional grounds, at the hands of a single federal district judge." This policy would not be undermined by narrowly interpreting section 1253 to include only "three-judge court orders that *grant* injunctions." Whether section 1253 should be so severely restricted, however, is a question that is unnecessary to decide this case.

"Here the three-judge court dismissed the complaint for lack of 'standing.'" A dismissal on that ground, however, could also have been issued by a single judge.

> It is now well settled that refusal to request the convention of a three-judge court, dissolution of a three-judge court, and dismissal of a complaint by a single judge are orders reviewable in the Court of Appeals, not here. If the three-judge court . . . had dissolved itself on grounds that "standing" was absent, and had left subsequent dismissal of the complaint to a single judge, this Court would thus clearly have lacked appellate jurisdiction over both orders. The same would have been true if the dissolution and dismissal decisions had been made simultaneously, with the single judge merely adopting the action of the three-judge court. The locus of appellate review should not turn on such technical distinctions. . . . We hold, therefore, that when a three-judge court denies a plaintiff injunctive relief on grounds which, if sound, would have justified dissolution of the court as to that plaintiff, or a refusal to request the convention of a three-judge court *ab initio*, review of the denial is available only in the Court of Appeals.

## *Warth* v. *Seldin*, 422 U.S. 490 (1975)

*Facts:* Three categories of plaintiffs brought suit seeking declaratory and injunctive relief and damages against the town of Penfield, New York. They alleged that Penfield's zoning ordinance, by its terms and as enforced, effectively excluded persons of low and moderate income from living in the town, in violation of several constitutional provisions. The first category of plaintiffs consisted of four persons with low or moderate incomes living in Rochester, New York, which is adjacent to Penfield. They alleged that the zoning laws of Penfield made it impossible for them to locate adequate housing there that was within their means. The second category of plaintiffs consisted of Rochester taxpayers. They alleged that the zoning practices of Penfield forced Rochester to subsidize a greater number of low-

and moderate-income housing units than it otherwise would, thereby increasing their tax burden. The third category of plaintiffs consisted of an association of home builders, which alleged that the allegedly unconstitutional zoning practices of Penfield precluded its members from building low- and moderate-income housing there. A lower federal court dismissed the complaint on the ground that all plaintiffs lacked standing to challenge the zoning ordinance of Penfield.

*Question:* Do all the plaintiffs lack standing?

*Decision:* Yes. Opinion by Justice Powell. Vote: 5–4, Douglas, Brennan, White, and Marshall dissenting.

*Reasons:* The opinion reasoned that

> in essence the question of standing is whether the litigant is entitled to have the court decide the merits of the dispute or of particular issues. This inquiry involves both constitutional limitations on federal court jurisdiction and prudential limitations on its exercise. . . . In both dimensions it is founded in concern about the proper—and properly limited —role of the courts in a democratic society.

Standing is an aspect of the restriction on federal judicial power in Article III of the Constitution to "cases" or "controversies." To obtain standing, a plaintiff must allege some distinct and palpable injury to himself which has been substantially caused by the defendant.

The first category of plaintiffs lacked standing because they failed to allege that their inability to locate suitable housing in Penfield resulted in any concretely demonstrable way from the town's allegedly unconstitutional actions. The availability to these plaintiffs of housing at low or moderate cost in Penfield has always depended on the efforts and willingness of third-party builders. The record is devoid of any indication that any such housing projects which Penfield rejected would have satisfied the needs of these plaintiffs at affordable prices or that they would benefit if the challenged zoning ordinance were held to be unconstitutional.

> In short, the facts alleged fail to support an actionable causal relationship between Penfield's zoning practices and . . . asserted injury [to the first plaintiff category]. . . . We hold only that a plaintiff who seeks to challenge exclusionary zoning practices must allege specific, concrete facts demonstrating that the challenged practices harm *him*, and that he personally would benefit in a tangible way from the courts' intervention. (Emphasis in original.)

The second category of plaintiffs failed to allege any realistic link between their increased taxes and Penfield's zoning ordinance. Such increases result from actions taken by Rochester authorities, who are not parties to this case. The basis of their claim, moreover, is that the constitutional rights of third parties, namely persons of low and moderate income, have been violated by the zoning practices of Penfield. Except in extraordinary circumstances, not present in this case, the requirement of standing bars a litigant from advancing the rights of others to obtain relief for himself.

The third category of plaintiffs lacked standing for failing to allege that any specific housing project of any of its members is currently precluded either by the challenged zoning ordinance or by the action of Penfield in enforcing it.

> There is no averment that any member has applied to [Penfield] for a building permit or a variance with respect to any current project. Indeed, there is no indication that [Penfield has] delayed or thwarted any project currently proposed by [the association's] members, or that any of its members has taken advantage of the remedial processes available under the ordinance. In short . . . [the home builders association] has failed to show the existence of any injury to its members of sufficient immediacy and ripeness to warrant judicial intervention.

## *Alyeska Pipeline Service Co. v. The Wilderness Society*, 421 U.S. 240 (1975)

*Facts:* The Wilderness Society and other environmental groups brought suit against the secretary of the interior to prevent the issuance of permits to Alyeska which were required for its construction of the trans-Alaskan oil pipeline. After Alyeska intervened to defend the suit, a federal court of appeals ruled that the permits were prohibited by the Mineral Leasing Act of 1920. (Congress then amended that act to allow issuance of the permits.)

Subsequently, the environmentalist groups recovered attorneys' fees from Alyeska. The court of appeals held that the environmentalist groups had acted to vindicate important statutory rights of all citizens; that they had ensured that the governmental system functioned properly; and that they were entitled to attorneys' fees lest the great cost of litigation of this kind, particularly against well-financed defendants such as Alyeska, deter private parties desiring to ensure that the laws protecting the environment were properly enforced.

*Question:* Were the environmentalist groups entitled to recover attorneys' fees against Alyeska?

*Decision:* No. Opinion by Justice White. Vote: 5–2, Brennan and Marshall dissenting. Douglas and Powell did not participate.

*Reasons:* "In the United States, the prevailing litigant is ordinarily not entitled to collect a reasonable attorneys' fee from the loser." Three judicially crafted exceptions to the rule, inapplicable to this case, however, have been established.

> [A] trustee of a fund or property, or a party preserving or recovering a fund for the benefit of others in addition to himself, [can] recover his costs, including his attorneys' fees, from the fund or property itself or directly from the other parties enjoying the benefit. . . . Also, a court may assess attorneys' fees for the "willful disobedience of a court order . . . as part of the fine to be levied on the defendant." . . . or when the losing party has "acted in bad faith, vexatiously, wantonly, or for oppressive reasons."

Federal statutes reflect an acceptance of this general rule against the allowance of attorneys' fees with these narrow exceptions: The statutes have not "extended any roving authority to the Judiciary to allow counsel fees as costs or otherwise whenever the courts might deem them warranted." Instead, Congress has made explicit provision for the allowance of attorneys' fees under selected statutes when it has intended to depart from the general rule.

> It appears to us that the rule suggested here and adopted by the Court of Appeals would make major inroads on a policy matter that Congress has reserved for itself. Since the approach taken by Congress to this issue has been to carve out specific exceptions to a general rule that federal courts cannot award attorneys' fees . . . those courts are not free to fashion drastic new rules with respect to the allowance of attorneys' fees to the prevailing party in federal litigation or to pick and choose among plaintiffs and the statutes under which they sue and to award fees in some cases but not in others, depending upon the courts' assessment of the importance of the public policies involved in particular cases.

### *Johnson* v. *Mississippi*, 421 U.S. 213 (1975)

*Facts:* Six Negro citizens were arrested and charged under Mississippi law for conspiring unlawfully to cause a boycott of certain business establishments. The Negroes had been picketing and urging a boycott of these businesses because of their alleged racial discrimination in employment. They unsuccessfully sought removal of the prosecution from state to federal court pursuant to 28 U.S.C. 1443(1). That section provides for removal of state criminal prosecutions to federal court in any case in which the defendant "is denied or cannot enforce in the courts of such State a right under any law providing for the equal civil rights of citizens of the United States."

*Question:* Were the Negro defendants entitled to remove their prosecution to federal court under 28 U.S.C. 1443(1)?

*Decision:* No. Opinion by Justice White. Vote: 6–2, Brennan and Marshall dissenting. Douglas did not participate.

*Reasons: Georgia* v. *Rachel,* 384 U.S. 780 (1966), and *City of Greenwood* v. *Peacock,* 384 U.S. 808 (1966), established that a removal petition under section 1443(1) must satisfy a two-pronged test.

> First, it must appear that the right allegedly denied the removal petitioner arises under a federal law "providing for specific civil rights stated in terms of racial equality." . . . Claims that prosecution and conviction will violate rights under constitutional or statutory provisions of general applicability or under statutes not protecting against racial discrimination, will not suffice.
>
> Second, it must appear, in accordance with the provisions of section 1443(1), that the removal petitioner is "denied or cannot enforce" the specified federal rights "in the courts of the State." This provision normally requires that the "denial be manifest in a formal expression of state law," . . . such as a state legislative or constitutional provision, "rather than a denial first made manifest in the trial of the case."

Here, it is claimed that removal is justified because the federal civil rights protected by 18 U.S.C. 245(b)(5) would be denied by the state prosecution. That section makes it a crime to interfere with or to intimidate any person by force or threats of force because of his participation in free speech or assembly opposing racial discrimination in employment.

Irrespective of whether section 245 provides for specific civil rights stated in terms of racial equality, Congress clearly did not intend that provision to justify interruption of state prosecutions.

> [Section 245] on its face focuses on the use of force, and its legislative history confirms that its central purpose was to prevent and punish *violent* interferences with the exercise of specified rights and that it was not aimed at interrupt-

ing or frustrating the otherwise orderly processes of state law. . . .

Viewed in this context, it seems quite evident that a state prosecution, proceeding as it does in a court of law, cannot be characterized as an application of "force or the threat of force" within the meaning of section 245. That section furnishes federal protection against violence in certain circumstances. But whatever "rights" it may confer, none of them is denied by a state criminal prosecution for conspiracy or boycott. (Emphasis in original.)

The Negro defendants had no federal statutory right that precluded the state from prosecuting them for their conduct.

## Sex Discrimination

Continuing a clear shift of judicial attitude toward claims of sex discrimination begun in 1971,[35] the Court decided four cases all favorably to women. It ruled that under the Constitution:

—A woman's right to serve as a juror may not be conditioned upon her filing a written application requesting jury service (*Taylor* v. *Louisiana*, 419 U.S. 522).

—A statute may not provide a lower age of majority for females than males for purposes of receiving child support (*Stanton* v. *Stanton*, 421 U.S. 7).

—Social security benefits based upon the earnings of a deceased spouse must be paid both to widows and widowers (*Weinberger* v. *Wiesenfeld*, 420 U.S. 636).

—Women could be judged by a more lenient standard than men in measuring their performance in the armed forces because their promotional opportunities were fewer. (*Schlesinger* v. *Ballard*, 419 U.S. 498).

In substantial part, these decisions reflect the enormous advances that women have made in education, business, and the professions and a lessened societal expectation that their lives will revolve mainly around the home. As Justice Blackmun noted in *Stanton* v. *Stanton*:

No longer is the female destined solely for the home and the rearing of the family, and only the male for the marketplace and the world of ideas. Women's activities and responsibilities are increasing and expanding. The presence of women

---

[35] See Reed v. Reed, 404 U.S. 71 (1971).

in business, in the professions, in government and, indeed, in all walks of life where education is a desirable, if not always a necessary antecedent, is apparent and a proper subject of judicial notice.

The Court has seemingly rejected Justice Frankfurter's statement in *Goesaert v. Cleary*, 335 U.S. 464 (1948), that although: [36]

women may now have achieved the virtues that men have long claimed as their prerogatives and now indulge in vices that men have long practiced . . . [t]he Constitution does not require legislatures to reflect sociological insight, or shifting social standards.

The current attitude of the Court toward women's rights contrasts sharply with its decisions a century ago. In *Bradwell v. Illinois*, 83 U.S. (16 Wall.) 130 (1873), the Court held that a state might constitutionally deny women the right to practice law. Mr. Justice Bradley, in a concurring opinion, asserted that the

harmony, not to say identity, of interests and views which belong or should belong to the family institution, is repugnant to the idea of a woman adopting a distinct and independent career from that of her husband. . . . The paramount destiny and mission of woman are to fulfill the noble and benign offices of wife and mother. This is the law of the Creator.

### *Taylor v. Louisiana*, 419 U.S. 522 (1975)

*Facts:* A male defendant was convicted of a crime in Louisiana state court by a petit jury chosen from a venire containing no women. He appealed, claiming that women were systematically excluded from the venire and that he was thus deprived of his federal constitutional right to a fair trial by jury drawn from a representative segment of the community.

Louisiana law provides that a woman should not be selected for jury service unless she has previously filed a written declaration of a desire for such service. Consequently, although females constituted 53 percent of the persons eligible for jury service in the district where the defendant was tried, no more than 10 percent of the persons on the jury wheel were women.

---

[36] There the Court upheld a Michigan statute prohibiting a female from obtaining a bartender's license unless she was the wife or daughter of the male owner of a licensed liquor establishment.

*Question:* Did the Louisiana jury selection system deprive the defendant of his Sixth Amendment right to an impartial jury?

*Decision:* Yes. Opinion by Justice White. Vote: 8–1, Rehnquist dissenting.

*Reasons:* In *Duncan* v. *Louisiana*, 391 U.S. 145 (1968), the Court held "that the Sixth Amendment's provision for jury trial is made binding on the States by virtue of the Fourteenth Amendment." Other decisions have made clear "that the selection of a petit jury from a representative cross section of the community is an essential component of the Sixth Amendment right to a jury trial." This requirement is necessary if the jury is to serve its basic purpose: to guard against the exercise of arbitrary power by making

> available the commonsense judgment of the community as a hedge against the overzealous or mistaken prosecutor and in preference to the professional or perhaps overconditioned or biased response of a judge. . . . This prophylactic vehicle is not provided if the jury pool is made up of only special segments of the populace or if large, distinctive groups are excluded from the pool.

The fair-cross-section requirement is violated by the systematic exclusion of women from jury service. As the Court noted in *Ballard* v. *United States*, 329 U.S. 187 (1946), the "two sexes are not fungible." A community composed of both sexes may be subject to subtle influences and possess a distinct though intangible quality that would be lacking in a community of one sex.

It is argued, nevertheless,

> that women as a class serve a distinctive role in society and that jury service would so substantially interfere with that function that the State has ample justification for excluding women from service unless they volunteer, even though the result is that almost all jurors are men. . . . [However], [i]t is untenable to suggest these days that it would be a special hardship for each and every woman to perform jury service or that society cannot spare *any* women from their present duties. This may be the case with many, and it may be burdensome to sort out those who should not be exempted from those who should serve. But that task is performed in the case of men, and the administrative convenience in dealing with women as a class is insufficient justification for diluting the quality of community judgment represented by the jury in criminal trials. (Emphasis in original.)

The Court concluded by observing that

> [i]f it was ever the case that women were unqualified to sit on juries or were so situated that none of them should be required to perform jury service, that time has long since passed. If at one time it could be held that Sixth Amendment juries must be drawn from a fair cross section of the community but that this requirement permitted the almost total exclusion of women, this is not the case today. Communities differ at different times and places. What is a fair cross section at one time or place is not necessarily a fair cross section at another time or a different place.

In a subsequent case, *Daniel* v. *Louisiana,* 420 U.S. 31 (1975), the Court held that *Taylor* should not be applied retroactively to convictions obtained by juries empanelled prior to the date of that decision.

## *Weinberger* v. *Wiesenfeld,* 420 U.S. 636 (1975)

*Facts:* Under section 402(g) of the Social Security Act, benefits based on the earnings of a deceased husband and father are generally payable both to the widow and to minor children in her care. Benefits based on the earnings of a deceased wife and mother, however, are payable only to the minor children and not to the widower. A three-judge federal court held section 402(g) unconstitutional on the ground that it unjustifiably discriminated against women wage earners by providing less protection for their survivors than it provided to male workers.

*Question:* Does section 402(g) unconstitutionally discriminate on the basis of sex in violation of the due process clause of the Fifth Amendment?

*Decision:* Yes. Opinion by Justice Brennan. Vote: 8–0. Douglas did not participate.

*Reasons:* The sex-based distinction made by section 402(g) is indistinguishable from that invalidated in *Frontiero* v. *Richardson,* 411 U.S. 677 (1973). There the Court struck down a statute which was more generous in providing benefits to the wife of a serviceman than to the husband of a servicewoman. *Frontiero* rejected the contention that the discrimination was justified by the assumption that

> "female spouses of servicemen would normally be dependent upon their husbands, while male spouses of servicewomen

would not." . . . A virtually identical "archaic and over-broad" generalization . . . "not . . . tolerated under the Constitution" underlies the distinction drawn by section 402(g), namely, that male workers' earnings are vital to the support of their families, while the earnings of female wage-earners do not significantly contribute to their families' support.

It is argued that the discrimination embodied in section 402(g) was intended to compensate

> women beneficiaries as a group for the economic difficulties which still confront women who seek to support themselves and their families. The Court held in *Kahn* v. *Shevin*, 416 U.S. 351 (1974), that a statute "reasonably designed to further a state policy of cushioning the financial impact of spousal loss upon that sex for which that loss imposes a disproportionately heavy burden" can survive an equal protection attack. . . . [However], it is apparent both from [the Social Security Act's] statutory scheme . . . and from the legislative history of section 402(g) that Congress' purpose in providing benefits to young widows with children was not to provide an income to women who were, because of economic discrimination, unable to provide for themselves. Rather, section 402 (g), linked as it is directly to responsibility for minor children, was intended to permit women to elect not to work and to devote themselves to the care of children. Since this purpose in no way is premised upon any special disadvantages of women, it cannot serve to justify a gender-based distinction which diminishes the protection afforded to women who do work.

### *Schlesinger* v. *Ballard*, 419 U.S. 498 (1975)

*Facts:* A male naval officer (Ballard) with more than nine years of active service twice failed to be selected for promotion and was thus mandatorily discharged under 10 U.S.C. 6382(a). He challenged the constitutionality of that statute on the ground that it invidiously discriminated against him on account of sex in violation of the due process clause of the Fifth Amendment. He reasoned that if he had been a woman officer, he would have been subject to a different separation statute, 10 U.S.C. 6401, which would have entitled him to thirteen years of commissioned service before a mandatory discharge for want of promotion.

*Question:* Is section 6382(a) constitutional as applied to Ballard?

*Decision:* Yes. Opinion by Justice Stewart. Vote: 5–4, Douglas, Brennan, White, and Marshall dissenting.

*Reasons:* The Court noted that

the different treatment of men and women naval officers under sections 6401 and 6382 reflects, not archaic and over-broad generalizations, but, instead, the demonstrable fact that male and female line officers in the Navy are *not* similarly situated with respect to opportunities for professional service. [Ballard] has not challenged the current restrictions on women officers' participation in combat and in most sea duty. . . . Thus, in competing for promotion, female lieutenants will not generally have compiled records of sea-going service comparable to those of male lieutenants. In enacting and retaining section 6401, Congress may thus quite rationally have believed that women line officers had less opportunity for promotion than did their male counterparts, and that a longer period of tenure for women officers would, therefore, be consistent with the goal to provide women officers with "fair and equitable career advancement programs." (Emphasis in original.)

The statutes in question operate to promote officers at a rate "commensurate with the Navy's current needs and [serve] to motivate qualified commissioned officers to so conduct themselves that they may realistically look forward to higher levels of command." They were enacted pursuant to the broad congressional and executive constitutional responsibilities to prepare the armed forces for combat. "We cannot say that, in exercising its broad constitutional power here, Congress has violated the Due Process Clause of the Fifth Amendment."

## *Stanton* v. *Stanton*, 421 U.S. 7 (1975)

*Facts:* Pursuant to a Utah divorce decree, a husband was ordered to pay child support for his seven-year-old daughter and five-year-old son. When the daughter reached eighteen, the age of majority for females under Utah law, the husband discontinued payments for her support. The wife brought suit to compel continuation of support payments to her daughter. She argued that the Utah statute, which provides that the age of majority is twenty-one for a male and eighteen for a female, was invidiously discriminatory in violation of the equal protection clause of the Fourteenth Amendment. The Utah Supreme Court rejected that argument, reasoning that the discrimination was justified because girls tend to mature before boys, girls tend to marry earlier than boys, and boys should receive a good education and training before undertaking their primary responsibilities to provide a home and its essentials.

*Question:* Is the challenged Utah statute unconstitutional insofar as it prescribes different ages of majority for males and females for purposes of receiving child support.

*Decision:* Yes. Opinion by Justice Blackmun. Vote: 8–1, Rehnquist dissenting.

*Reasons:* The question in this case "is whether the difference in sex between children warrants the distinction in the [husband's] obligation to support that is drawn by the Utah statute." The distinction is wholly unrelated to the objective of that statute.

> A child, male or female, is still a child. "No longer is the female destined solely for the home and the rearing of the family, and only the male for the marketplace and the world of ideas. . . . Women's activities and responsibilities are increasing and expanding. Coeducation is a fact, not a rarity. The presence of women in business, in the professions, in government and, indeed, in all walks of life where education is a desirable, if not always a necessary antecedent, is apparent and a proper subject of judicial notice. If a specified age of minority is required for the boy in order to assure him parental support while he attains his education and training, so, too, it is for the girl. To distinguish between the two on educational grounds is to be self-serving: if the female is not to be supported so long as the male, she hardly can be expected to attend school as long as he does, and bringing her education to an end earlier coincides with the role-typing society has long imposed. And if any weight remains in this day in the claim of earlier maturity of the female, with a concomitant inference of absence of need for support beyond 18, we fail to perceive its unquestioned truth or its significance, particularly when marriage, as the statute provides, terminates minority for a person of either sex.

Accordingly, the challenged Utah statute violates the equal protection clause.

## Antitrust

In its past two terms, the antitrust decisions of the Court have charted a clear probusiness course. The current antitrust philosophy of the

Court stands in sharp contrast to that underlying several Warren Court decisions.[37] Whereas the Warren Court seemed to assume anticompetitive effects from most mergers, the present Court appears willing to find an absence of anticompetitive effects in light of special circumstances.[38] The Warren Court also inferred immunity from the antitrust laws much less readily than the present Court.[39] This term, the Court decided five antitrust cases favorable to business. At issue in its most important case was whether certain agreements between the National Association of Securities Dealers and others respecting the sale of mutual funds were implicitly immune from antitrust attack by virtue of statutes regulating the sale of such securities. By a 5–4 vote, the Court appeared to adopt the doctrine that private agreements, subject to only general supervision by a regulatory authority, are generally immune from the antitrust laws. That doctrine seems to be at odds with the pronouncement of the Court, made more than a decade ago, that statutes should not be construed to repeal the antitrust laws by implication unless that construction is clearly compelled. *Silver v. New York Stock Exchange*, 373 U.S. 341 (1963). The new attitude of the Court toward antitrust immunity may protect numerous business practices subject to some type of regulation.

In a bank merger case, the Court implied that mergers are not barred by the Clayton Act if there is evidence that the merging companies do not wish to compete. The Court appeared to reject the assumption that in the long term, independent business competitors will compete in the absence of collusion.

The Court narrowed the application of the Clayton and Robinson-Patman acts in concluding that they reached transactions in the direct flow of interstate commerce but not transactions which merely "affected" interstate commerce.

In an important antitrust victory for consumers, the Court unanimously ruled that state and local bar associations could not enforce minimum fee schedules for title searches. The Court thereby

---

[37] See Pabst Brewing Co. v. U.S., 384 U.S. 546 (1966); U.S. v. Von's Grocery Co., 384 U.S. 270 (1966); FTC v. Procter and Gamble Co., 386 U.S. 568 (1967); U.S. v. Philadelphia National Bank, 374 U.S. 371 (1963); Silver v. New York Stock Exchange, 373 U.S. 341 (1963); Fortner Enterprises, Inc. v. U.S. Steel Corp., 394 U.S. 495 (1969).

[38] Compare U.S. v. Von's Grocery Co., 384 U.S. 270 (1966), and Pabst Brewing Co. v. U.S., 384 U.S. 270 (1966) with U.S. v. General Dynamics Corp., 415 U.S. 486 (1974) and U.S. v. Marine Bancorporation Inc., 418 U.S. 602 (1974).

[39] Compare U.S. v. Philadelphia National Bank, 374 U.S. 321 (1963), and Silver v. New York Stock Exchange, 373 U.S. 341 (1963) with U.S. v. N.A.S.D., 422 U.S. 694 (1975).

concluded that the professions are not exempt from the antitrust laws. Its decision indicated that a profession which restricts advertising among its members and adheres to other anticompetitive practices may be in violation of the Sherman Act.

Unlike business, unions were unsuccessful in claiming antitrust immunity in an important decision for the construction industry. Narrowly interpreting statutes which expressly granted unions certain antitrust immunity, the Court held illegal, under the Sherman Act, picketing by construction unions for the purpose of compelling general contractors to subcontract work only to employers who had contracts with such unions.

## United States v. National Association of Securities Dealers, Inc., 422 U.S. 694 (1975)

*Facts:* The United States brought suit against the National Association of Securities Dealers (NASD), certain mutual funds, mutual fund underwriters, and securities broker-dealers. It alleged that these groups violated section 1 of the Sherman Act by entering into agreements restricting and fixing the resale price of mutual-fund shares in secondary market transactions between dealers, from an investor to a dealer, and between investors through brokered transactions. The defendants claimed that the challenged agreements were immune from antitrust liability on the ground that they were already subject to comprehensive regulation by the Securities and Exchange Commission under the Maloney Act and the Investment Company Act of 1940.

*Question:* Are the challenged agreements immune from antitrust liability?

*Decision:* Yes. Opinion by Justice Powell. Vote: 5-4, Douglas, Brennan, White, and Marshall dissenting.

*Reasons:* Section 22 of the Investment Company Act of 1940 was enacted to prevent underwriters and dealers in mutual funds from using their expert knowledge of the market to the disadvantage of public investors. To help achieve this goal, section 22(d) prohibits mutual funds and dealers from selling shares to the public at other than the public-offering price. That prohibition, however, does not sanction the agreement between the defendants to refuse to act as a broker or dealer in any sale of mutual funds in the secondary market at other than the current public-offering price. But section 22(f) authorizes mutual funds to impose restrictions on the transferability of their shares provided that they are stated in its registration statement and do not contravene any rules issued by the Securities and Exchange Commission (SEC) to protect shareholders. All but one of the challenged restrictive agreements were noted in registration statements and did not violate any SEC rules. These agreements are immune from the antitrust laws because section 22(f) reflects a clear congressional determination that, subject to SEC oversight, mutual funds should be allowed to restrict the transferability of shares. The SEC has not neglected its oversight responsibilities. "[Its] acceptance of fund-initiated restrictions for more than three decades . . . manifests an informed administrative judgment that the contractual restrictions employed by the funds to protect their shareholders were appropriate means for combatting the problems of the industry."

The one agreement unprotected by section 22(f) operated to discourage NASD members from developing a secondary dealer market and brokerage market in transactions involving shares in mutual funds. This agreement, however, consisted of rules established by the NASD in its self-regulatory function as authorized by the Maloney Act. That act confers comprehensive supervisory authority on the SEC, which is required to approve or reject NASD rules, as necessary, to protect the public interest and the interests of shareholders. "[T]he investiture of such pervasive supervisory authority in the SEC suggests that Congress intended to lift the ban of the Sherman Act from [NASD] activities approved by the SEC."

The Court asserted that its decision was consistent with *Silver* v. *New York Stock Exchange,* 373 U.S. 341 (1963), which held that restrictions on competition under the securities laws are immune from antitrust attack only to the extent necessary to make the regulatory scheme established by those laws function properly.

## *United States* v. *Citizens and Southern National Bank,* 422 U.S. 86 (1975)

*Facts:* To circumvent Georgia's restrictions on branch banking, Citizens and Southern National Bank, located in Atlanta, formed a holding company (C & S). C & S embarked on a program of forming de facto branch banks in the suburbs of Atlanta. This program involved, among other features, ownership by C & S of 5 percent of the stock of each of the suburban banks, ownership of much of the remaining stock by parties friendly to C & S, use by the suburban banks of the C & S logogram and of all of C & S's banking services, and close C & S oversight of the operation and governance of the suburban banks.

In 1970, Georgia amended its banking statutes to allow de jure branching on a countywide basis. C & S consequently applied to the Federal Deposit Insurance Corporation (FDIC), under the Bank Merger Act of 1966, for permission to acquire all of the stock of six of the 5 percent banks historically operated by C & S as de facto branches. The FDIC authorized all but one of the proposed acquisitions.

The Justice Department brought suit under the antitrust laws against C & S and its related banking entities. It alleged that the five acquisitions authorized by the FDIC would lessen competition in relevant banking markets, thus violating section 7 of the Clayton Act, and that the historic, "de facto branch" relations between C & S and the six 5 percent banks constituted unreasonable restraints of trade in violation of section 1 of the Sherman Act. After a trial, a federal district court rendered judgment for C & S on all the issues.

*Question:* Was the federal district court decision correct?

*Decision:* Yes. Opinion by Justice Stewart. Vote: 6–3, Brennan, Douglas, and White dissenting.

*Reasons:* With respect to the Sherman Act, the government contends that the relationships between C & S and the six 5 percent banks constituted unreasonable restraints of trade on two alternate theories:

> (1) The relationships encompassed an agreement to fix interest rates and service charges among the 5-percent banks, and between these banks and C & S-owned banks, resulting in a "per se" violation of the Sherman Act. (2) The programs unreasonably restrained interbank competition, as to prices and services, by extending interbank cooperation far beyond the conventional "correspondent" arrangements which large city banks traditionally make with small banks in outlying markets.

These contentions lack merit for two basic reasons.

First, under the Bank Holding Company Act Amendments of 1966, 12 U.S.C. 1849(d), any bank "acquisition, merger, or consolidation" consummated prior to July 1, 1966, and which was unchallenged by the attorney general on that date is immune from antitrust attack under section 1 of the Sherman Act. Three of the C & S 5 percent de facto branch banks were formed before July 1966. While this formation was a unique type of transaction, it may fairly be characterized as an "acquisition, merger, or consolidation" within the meaning of section 1849(d). The formation

> involved the direct and indirect acquisition of bank stock, and the direct and indirect assertion of control over the governance and operations of a bank, by a bank holding company. Though unusual in form, such a transaction quite clearly falls within the class of dealings by bank holding companies which Congress intended, in section 1849(d), to shield from retroactive challenge under the antitrust laws.

Second, the three 5 percent banks formed after July 1966 were "founded *ab initio* through the sponsorship of C & S." It is conceded that C & S regularly notified these banks of the interest rates and service charges in force at its affiliate banks and that the rates and charges of all these banks were generally uniform.

> Were we dealing with independent competitors having no permissible reason for intimate and continuous cooperation and consultation as to almost every facet of doing business, the evidence adduced here might well preclude a finding that the parties were not engaged in a conspiracy to affect prices. But, [since] the correspondent associate program, as such, was permissible under the Sherman Act . . . we cannot hold clearly erroneous the District Court's finding that the lack of significant price competition did not flow from a tacit agreement but instead was an indirect, unintentional, and formally discouraged result of the sharing of expertise and information which was at the heart of the correspondent associate program.

The correspondent associate programs were reasonable under the Sherman Act. They were established as a direct response to Georgia's historic restrictions on de jure branching. "To characterize these relationships as an unreasonable restraint of trade is to forget that their whole purpose and effect were to *defeat* a restraint of trade. Georgia's antibranching law amounted to a compulsory market division." The suggestion by the government that a less intimate correspondent relationship between C & S and the 5 percent banks would have been equally procompetitive and would have had the added virtue of facilitating competition among the 5 percent banks is mere speculation.

The issue under the Clayton Act is whether the effect of the proposed acquisitions, approved by the FDIC, "may be substantially to lessen competition . . . in any line of commerce in any section of the country." The district court concluded that C & S had made the necessary showing that these proposed acquisitions would not "lessen" competition for the simple reason that under the correspondent associate program that had been continuously in effect, no real competition had developed or was likely to develop among the 5 percent banks. With respect to future competition, the district court failed to find any realistic prospect that denial of these acquisitions would lead the defendant banks to compete against each other. These findings were not "clearly erroneous." Thus, the Clayton Act claim must be rejected for failure to show that the challenged acquisition would have the "probable" effect of lessening competition.

### *Connell Construction Co. Inc.* v. *Plumbers and Steamfitters, Local No. 100*, 421 U.S. 616 (1975)

*Facts:* A union representing the plumbing and mechanical trades had a multiemployer collective-bargaining agreement with an association of mechanical contractors. The agreement contained a "most-favored-nation" clause which provided that if the union granted a more favorable contract to any other member it would extend the same terms to the members of the association. The union picketed a general building contractor (Connell) for the sole purpose of compelling Connell to agree that it would subcontract mechanical work only to employers who had contracts with the union. After signing such an agreement under protest, Connell sued the union, alleging its invalidity on the grounds that it violated the Sherman Antitrust Act and state antitrust laws. A federal district court held that the agreement was exempt from the Sherman Act because it was authorized by the construction industry proviso to section 8(e) of the National Labor Relations Act (NLRA) and that federal labor legislation preempted the antitrust laws of the state.

*Questions:* (1) Was the agreement exempt from the Sherman Act? (2) Were the state's antitrust laws preempted by the federal labor law?

*Decision:* No to the first question and yes to the second. Opinion by Justice Powell. Vote: 5–4 on the first question, Douglas, Brennan, Stewart, and Marshall dissenting, and 9–0 on the second.

*Reasons:* The Clayton Act and the Norris–La Guardia Act "declare that labor unions are not combinations or conspiracies in restraint of trade, and exempt specific union activities, including secondary picketing and boycotts, from the operation of the antitrust laws." The Court has ruled, however, that this exemption does not cover agreements between a union and a nonlabor party which restrains competition in the business market. Such agreements are lawful only to the extent necessary to eliminate competition over wages and working conditions.

Here, the challenged agreement

> indiscriminately excluded nonunion subcontractors from a portion of the market, even if their competitive advantages were not derived from substandard wages and working conditions but rather from more efficient operating methods. Curtailment of competition based on efficiency is neither a goal of federal labor policy nor a necessary effect of the elimination of competition among workers. Moreover, competition based on efficiency is a positive value that the antitrust laws strive to protect.

The effect of the challenged agreement was to eliminate competition among subcontractors on all subjects covered by the union's multi-employer agreement, even those unrelated to wages or working conditions. "The federal policy favoring collective bargaining therefore can offer no shelter for the union's coercive action against Connell or its campaign to exclude nonunion firms from the subcontracting market."

It was contended, nevertheless, that section 8(e) of the NLRA protected the agreement from antitrust scrutiny on the theory that it authorizes any agreement in the construction industry relating to subcontracting of work to be done at the site of the construction. The legislative history of section 8(e), however, indicates that it was intended only to cover agreements arising from collective-bargaining relationships, and in this case the union had no collective-bargaining agreement with Connell. A contrary construction "would give construction unions an almost unlimited organizational weapon. The unions would be free to enlist any general contractor to bring economic pressure on nonunion subcontractors, as long as the agreement recited that it only covered work to be performed on some jobsite somewhere."

Finally, it was argued that, assuming the illegality of the agreement under section 8(e), antitrust remedies were inapplicable because the NLRA sanctions for such conduct are exclusive. "There is no legislative history, [however], suggesting that labor-law remedies for section 8(e) violations were intended to be exclusive, or that Congress thought allowing antitrust remedies in cases like the present one would be inconsistent with the remedial scheme of the NLRA."

Unlike the federal antitrust laws, state antitrust laws as applied to union activity closely related to organizational goals are preempted by the NLRA.

> Congress and this Court have carefully tailored the [federal] antitrust statutes to avoid conflict with the labor policy favoring lawful employee organization, not only by delineating exemptions from antitrust coverage but also by adjusting the scope of the antitrust remedies themselves. [In contrast], [s]tate antitrust laws . . . [i]f they take account of labor goals at all, . . . may represent a totally different balance between labor and antitrust policies. Permitting state antitrust law to operate in this field could frustrate the basic federal policies favoring employee organization and allowing elimination of competition among wage earners, and interfere with the detailed system Congress has created for regulating organizational techniques.

## *Goldfarb* v. *Virginia State Bar*, 421 U.S. 773 (1975)

*Facts:* Purchasers of a home in Fairfax County, Virginia, were informed by nineteen different attorneys that the fee they would charge for a title search would be 1 percent of the value of the property involved. That was the same charge suggested in a minimum-fee schedule published by the Fairfax County Bar Association. Enforcement of the fee schedule was provided by the Virginia State Bar, an administrative agency through which the Virginia Supreme Court regulates the practice of law. The state bar issued an ethical opinion stating that "evidence that an attorney *habitually* charges less than the suggested minimum fee schedule adopted by his local bar association raises a presumption that such lawyer is guilty of misconduct." (Emphasis in original.)

The purchasers brought a class action against the state and county bars alleging that the operation of the minimum-fee schedule, as applied to fees for legal services relating to residential real-estate transactions, constitutes price fixing in violation of section 1 of the Sherman Act. The court of appeals concluded that the actions of the state bar were immune from antitrust attack under the "state action" doctrine of *Parker* v. *Brown*, 317 U.S. 341 (1943); that the Sherman Act was inapplicable to the county bar because the practice of law is not "trade or commerce"; and that residential title searches had insufficient effect on interstate commerce to trigger application of the Sherman Act.

*Question:* Did the actions of the state bar and county bar in establishing and enforcing minimum-fee schedules for residential title searches constitute price fixing in violation of the Sherman Act?

*Decision:* Yes. Opinion by Chief Justice Burger. Vote: 8–0. Powell did not participate.

*Reasons:* It is clear that the fee schedule and its enforcement mechanism "constitute a classic illustration of price fixing." The fee schedule leads to a rigid price floor for title searches. It "was enforced through the prospect of professional discipline from the State Bar, and the desire of attorneys to comply with announced professional norms; the motivation to conform was reinforced by the assurance that other lawyers would not compete by underbidding."

The fee schedule also restrained interstate commerce within the meaning of the Sherman Act. A significant amount of mortgage money for homes purchased in Fairfax County comes from outside Virginia. Although title searches are performed wholly within the state, as a practical matter, they are necessary to interstate mortgage transactions which generally will not be consummated unless the borrower obtains a title examination. "Given the substantial volume of commerce involved, and the inseparability of this particular legal service from the interstate aspects of real estate transactions we conclude that interstate commerce has been sufficiently affected."

It is argued that the sale of legal services is exempt from the provisions of the Sherman Act because it was not intended to cover the learned professions. Neither the language, legislative history, nor purposes of the act support that contention. "Whatever else it may be, the examination of a land title is a service; the exchange of such a service for money is 'commerce' in the most common usage of that word. It is no disparagement of the practice of law as a profession to acknowledge that it has this business aspect, and [is subject to] the Sherman Act."

The fee schedule was also unprotected by the doctrine of *Parker* v. *Brown.* There the Court held that activity compelled by a state acting as a sovereign was immune from the Sherman Act. Here, however, no state law required maintenance of the challenged fee schedule. In addition, there is no indication that the Virginia Supreme Court approved of the ethical opinions of the state bar which encouraged adherence to the schedule. To fall within the protection of *Parker* v. *Brown,* "[i]t is not enough that . . . anticompetitive conduct is 'prompted' by state action; rather, anticompetitive activities must be compelled by direction of the State acting as a sovereign."

## United States v. American Building Maintenance Industries, 422 U.S. 271 (1975)

*Facts:* The United States brought suit against a large interstate supplier of janitorial services (American Building) alleging that it violated section 7 of the Clayton Act by acquiring two small janitorial service companies operating solely in southern California. Section 7 prohibits any corporation "engaged in commerce" from acquiring another corporation "engaged also in commerce" if the acquisition might substantially lessen competition or tend to create a monopoly. A federal district court dismissed the suit on the ground that the acquired companies were not "engaged in commerce" within the meaning of section 7.

*Question:* Was the dismissal proper?

*Decision:* Yes. Opinion by Justice Stewart. Vote: 6–3, Douglas, Brennan, and Blackmun dissenting.

*Reasons:* The phrase " 'in commerce' [in section 7] appears to denote only persons or activities within the flow of interstate commerce—the practical, economic continuity in the generation of goods and services for interstate markets and their transport and distribution to the consumer." That conclusion is supported by legislative history and prior court decisions interpreting that phrase in other statutes. "Accordingly, we hold that the phrase 'engaged in commerce' as used in section 7 of the Clayton Act means engaged in the flow of interstate commerce, and was not intended to reach all corporations engaged in activities subject to the federal commerce power."

In this case, the acquired companies "were completely insulated from any direct participation in interstate markets or the interstate flow of goods and services." The janitorial services of the two firms were provided and their supplies were purchased in transactions taking place entirely within the state. The fact that the firms provided localized services to other corporations engaged in interstate commerce did not satisfy the "in commerce" requirement of section 7. "In short, since the [acquired] companies did not participate directly in the sale, purchase, or distribution of goods or services in interstate commerce, they were not 'engaged in commerce' within the meaning of section 7 of the Clayton Act."

In a related case, *Gulf Oil Corp.* v. *Copp Paving Co.*, 419 U.S. 186 (1974), the Court also held that the Robinson-Patman Act applied to transactions "in commerce" but did not reach commercial activity which only "affected" interstate commerce.

## Labor Law

Two of the three significant labor law cases decided this term strengthened the power of unions. In *National Labor Relations Board v. J. Weingarten, Inc.*, 420 U.S. 251, the Court concluded that an employee under company investigation for misconduct has a right to the presence of a union representative while being interrogated by a company investigator. In *Emporium Capwell Co. v. Western Addition Community Organization*, 420 U.S. 50, the Court ruled that employees have no right to bypass union-management grievance procedures in order to protest alleged racial discrimination.

A union was unsuccessful, however, in *Muniz v. Hoffman*, 422 U.S. 454, in claiming either a statutory or constitutional right to jury trial on charges of criminal contempt stemming from its violation of an injunction issued under the National Labor Relations Act.

### *NLRB v. J. Weingarten, Inc.*, 420 U.S. 251 (1975)

*Facts:* An employee, under investigation by her employer for theft, requested the presence of a union representative while being interrogated by a company investigator. The request was denied, and the employee subsequently confessed to taking free lunches. The union filed a charge of unfair labor practice with the National Labor Relations Board (NLRB). It successfully contended that the employer's denial of the employee's request for the presence of her union representative at the investigatory interview, which she reasonably believed might result in disciplinary action, violated section 8(a)(1) of the National Labor Relations Act. The NLRB reasoned that the denial interfered with the employee's right under section 7 of the act "to engage in . . . concerted activities for . . . mutual aid or protection."

*Question:* Did the NLRB properly conclude that an employer's refusal to permit the presence of a union representative during an interview with an employee, who reasonably fears that it may result in disciplinary action, constitutes an unfair labor practice?

*Decision:* Yes. Opinion by Justice Brennan. Vote: 6–3, Burger, Powell, and Stewart dissenting.

*Reasons:* The NLRB has the "special function of applying general provisions of the Act to the complexities of industrial life." Accordingly, courts should defer to determinations by the NLRB unless they "run contrary to the language and tenor of the Act."

Although the NLRB's construction of the act may not be required, it "is at least permissible under it. . . ."

> The action of an employee in seeking to have the assistance of his union representative at a confrontation with his employer clearly falls within the literal wording of section 7 that "[e]mployees shall have the right . . . to engage in . . . concerted activities for the purpose of mutual aid or protection." . . . The union representative whose participation he seeks is . . . safeguarding not only the particular employee's interest but also the interests of the entire bargaining unit by exercising vigilance to make certain that the employer does not initiate or continue a practice of imposing punishment unjustly.

Thus, the presence of a union representative during an investigative interview constitutes concerted activity for mutual aid and protection within the meaning of section 7.

Moreover, the NLRB's construction of section 7 effectuates a fundamental purpose of the act: elimination of the inequality of bargaining power between employees and employers. "Requiring a lone employee to attend an investigative interview which he reasonably believes may result in the imposition of discipline perpetuates [this] inequality . . . and bars recourse to the safeguards the Act designed 'to redress the perceived imbalance of economic power between labor and management.' "

## *Emporium Capwell Co.* v. *Western Addition Community Organization*, 420 U.S. 50 (1975)

*Facts:* A union investigated the claim of employees that they were the victims of racial discrimination by their employer. Finding merit to the claim, the union invoked the grievance procedure in its collective-bargaining agreement by demanding that the joint union-management adjustment board "hear the entire case." Because processing individual grievances was thought inadequate to eliminate racial discrimination, certain employees picketed the employer's store in furtherance of their demand that the employer bargain directly with them about their grievances.

After being discharged for their activity, these employees filed a charge of unfair labor practice with the National Labor Relations

Board. They alleged that their picketing and their demand constituted concerted activity protected by section 7 of the National Labor Relations Act. In rejecting the claim, the NLRB reasoned that the activity of the employees was unprotected because it represented an attempt to circumvent the exclusive right of the union under the act to bargain with the employer over terms and conditions of employment.

The court of appeals reversed and remanded. It reasoned that concerted activity against racial discrimination enjoys a "unique status" under the act and under Title VII of the Civil Rights Act of 1964; that a union has a duty in cases such as this to seek to remedy the alleged discrimination to the fullest extent possible by the most expeditious and efficacious means; and that failure of a union to do so would authorize concerted activity by the minority group under section 7.

*Question:* Did the court of appeals err in reversing the decision of the NLRB?

*Decision:* Yes. Opinion by Justice Marshall. Vote: 8–1, Douglas dissenting.

*Reasons:* Section 9(a) of the act authorizes a union selected by a majority of employees in an appropriate unit to act as their exclusive bargaining agent with respect to terms and conditions of employment. "In establishing a regime of majority rule, Congress sought to secure to all members of the unit the benefits of their collective strength and bargaining power, in full awareness that the superior strength of some individuals or groups might be subordinated to the interest of the majority."

To prevent a "tyranny of majority over minority interests," however, the Court has held unions to a statutory duty to represent the interests of minorities fairly.

The fact that charges of racial discrimination are made does not justify departing from the exclusive representation principle in section 9(a). A union has a legitimate interest in presenting a united front in such cases "and in not seeing its strength dissipated and its stature denigrated by subgroups within the unit separately pursuing what they see as separate interests." Moreover, fragmentation of the bargaining unit is unnecessary to insure compliance with the strong national labor policy against racial discrimination. Accordingly, the attempt of the employees to "short-circuit" the union's orderly process for eliminating racial discrimination was unprotected concerted activity under section 7 of the act.

## *Muniz* v. *Hoffman*, 422 U.S. 454 (1975)

*Facts:* A labor union was found by a judge to be guilty of criminal contempt for violating a temporary injunction against picketing an employer that was issued under the authority of section 10(l) of the National Labor Relations Act. (Section 10[l] authorizes such injunctions to maintain the status quo pending final disposition of a charge of unfair labor practice against an employer by the National Labor Relations Board.) The union was fined $10,000. It appealed on the ground that its request for a jury trial was improperly denied. The union claimed a right to jury trial under 18 U.S.C. 3692, and by virtue of the Sixth Amendment.

*Question:* Did the union have either a statutory or a constitutional right to a jury trial on the criminal contempt charge?

*Decision:* No. Opinion by Justice White. Vote: 5–4, Douglas, Stewart, Marshall, and Powell dissenting.

*Reasons:* On its face, section 3692

> provides for jury trial in contempt cases arising under any federal law governing the issuance of injunctions in *any case* growing out of a labor dispute. . . . But it is not unusual that exceptions to the applicability of a statute's otherwise all-inclusive language are not contained in the enactment itself but are found in another statute dealing with particular situations to which the first statute might otherwise apply. (Emphasis in original.)

The crucial issue in this case is whether Congress intended to exempt proceedings to enforce injunctions under section 10(l) of the act from the provisions of section 3692 for a jury trial. The legislative history of section 10(l) and related provisions of the act make it reasonably clear that Congress intended this result.

The union also lacked a right to a jury trial under the Sixth Amendment. A series of recent decisions has established the following principles regarding a right to jury trial for criminal contempt:

> (1) Like other minor crimes, "petty" contempts may be tried without a jury, but contemnors in serious contempt cases in the federal system have a Sixth Amendment right to a jury trial; (2) criminal contempt, in and of itself and without regard for the punishment imposed, is not a serious offense absent legislative declaration to the contrary; (3) lacking legislative authorization of more serious punishment, a sen-

tence of as much as six months in prison, plus normal periods of probation, may be imposed without a jury trial; (4) but imprisonment for longer than six months is constitutionally impermissible unless the contemnor has been given the opportunity for a jury trial.

Here, the question raised is

whether a fine of $10,000 against an unincorporated labor union found guilty of criminal contempt may be imposed after denying the union's claim that it was entitled to a jury trial under the Sixth Amendment. . . . [We] cannot say that the fine of $10,000 imposed on [the union] in this case was a deprivation of such magnitude that a jury should have been interposed to guard against bias or mistake.

## Regulation of Business

The Court decided two important securities cases adversely to stockholders. It ruled in *United Housing Foundation* v. *Forman*, 421 U.S. 837, that stock purchased in a housing cooperative corporation, in order to obtain a place to live, is not a "security" entitled to the protections of the Securities Act of 1933 or the Securities Exchange Act of 1934.

Rule 10b-5, promulgated pursuant to the Securities Exchange Act, generally makes it unlawful to make false or misleading statements "in connection with the purchase or sale of a security." At issue in *Blue Chip Stamps* v. *Manor Drug Stores*, 427 U.S. 723, was whether a person who *declined* to purchase stock because of false or misleading statements could bring a private damage action under Rule 10b-5. By a vote of 6–3, the Court concluded that only purchasers or sellers of stock could sue for damages under that rule. Its decision rested in part on the practical difficulties of proving whether a failure to buy or sell stock was caused substantially by a false or misleading statement or, instead, by numerous other factors.

In the area of admiralty law, the Court joined the current trend in state law to apportion damages in tort suits on the basis of comparative negligence.[40] Some twenty-seven states have now adopted rules of comparative negligence. In *United States* v. *Reliable Transfer Co.*, 421 U.S. 397, the Court adopted a rule of comparative

---

[40] Under traditional negligence law, contributory negligence of a plaintiff bars him from recovery even if the defendant were more negligent than the plaintiff. Under comparative negligence law, negligence of a plaintiff, at least if less than that of the defendant, reduces, but does not bar, recovery.

negligence for collisions between vessels, overturning a century-old rule requiring equal division of damages between any parties at fault, no matter what the degree of fault.

The basic copyright law in the United States was enacted in 1909, long before radio and cable television were commonplace in households. Issues of copyright infringement involving entertainment provided through these media of communications have revealed the general inadequacy of the 1909 Copyright Act. In *Fortnightly Corp. v. United Artists*, 392 U.S. 390 (1968), and *Teleprompter Corp. v. Columbia Broadcasting System, Inc.*, 415 U.S. 394 (1974), the Court rejected the claim that cable operators commit copyright infringement when they intercept copyrighted TV programs and rechannel them to paying subscribers. This term, in *Twentieth Century Music Corp. v. Aiken*, 422 U.S. 151, the Court concluded that commercial businesses may install radio speakers to enable customers to listen to the radio without fear of copyright infringement. These cases have helped stimulate Congress to undertake reform of the copyright laws in light of today's technological and business environment.[41]

## *Blue Chip Stamps* v. *Manor Drug Stores*, 427 U.S. 723 (1975)

*Facts:* As required by an antitrust decree, New Blue Chip Stamp Company (Blue Chip) offered to sell its stock to certain retailers who had used Blue Chip stamps in the past. A retailer (Manor Drug) that had declined to purchase the stock sued Blue Chip two years later, alleging that the prospectus prepared and distributed by Blue Chip in connection with the offering was materially misleading in its unduly pessimistic appraisal of its financial status and prospects and that the failure of Manor Drug to purchase the offered stock was in reliance on the misleading prospectus. Manor Drug sought damages for the lost opportunity under Rule 10b-5 promulgated pursuant to the Securities Exchange Act. That rule makes it unlawful for any person through the use of an instrument of interstate commerce to make any untrue statement of material fact "in connection with the purchase or sale of a security." A federal district court dismissed the complaint on the ground that Rule 10b-5 authorizes a person to bring a private damage action only if he either purchased or sold a security.

---

[41] See P.L. 94-553. It provides, *inter alia*, for a jukebox royalty of $8 a machine a year, and for compulsory licensing of cable television systems to transmit programs broadcast by stations licensed by the Federal Communications Commission at prescribed royalty rates.

*Question:* Did the district court properly dismiss the Rule 10b-5 suit?

*Decision:* Yes. Opinion by Justice Rehnquist. Vote: 6–3, Blackmun, Brennan, and Douglas dissenting.

*Reasons:* In *Birnbaum* v. *Newport Steel Corp.*, 193 F.2d 461 (2d Cir. 1951), the second circuit concluded that the plaintiff class in a Rule 10b-5 action was limited to actual purchasers and sellers. Hundreds of lower federal court decisions have reaffirmed the *Birnbaum* conclusion over the past quarter century.

> In 1957 and again in 1959, the Securities and Exchange Commission sought from Congress amendment of section 10(b) to change its wording from "in connection with the purchase or sale of any security" to "in connection with the purchase or sale of, *or any attempt to purchase or sell,* any security.". . .
>
> The longstanding acceptance by the courts, coupled with Congress' failure to reject *Birnbaum's* reasonable interpretation of the wording of section 10(b), wording which is directed towards injury suffered "in connection with the purchase or sale" of securities, argues significantly in favor of acceptance of the *Birnbaum* rule by this Court. . . .
>
> Available extrinsic evidence from the texts of the 1933 [Securities Act] and 1934 [Securities Exchange Act] as to the congressional scheme in this regard, though not conclusive, supports the result reached by the *Birnbaum* court. (Emphasis in original.)

Nevertheless, because the congressional intent as to the contours of a private cause of action under Rule 10b-5 is unclear, it is proper to consider policy factors which argue for or against adoption of the *Birnbaum* rule.

The main disadvantage of the rule is that it may prevent some deserving plaintiffs from recovering damages which have in fact been caused by violations of Rule 10b-5.

Adoption of the rule, however, guards against the danger of vexatious litigation. Its absence would make dismissal of an unfounded Rule 10b-5 action based upon a failure to purchase or sell stock prior to trial difficult. This is because most such cases will turn largely upon conflicting oral testimony about a series of occurrences. Thus, without the *Birnbaum* rule there would be a large incentive for nonpurchasers or nonsellers to bring frivolous Rule 10b-5 suits because of their settlement value. Their pendency may frustrate or delay normal business activity of the defendant which is totally unrelated to the lawsuit.

In addition,

> abolition of the *Birnbaum* rule would throw open to the trier
> of fact many rather hazy issues of historical fact the proof
> of which depended almost entirely on oral testimony. . . .
> [B]ystanders to the securities marketing process could await
> developments on the sidelines without risk, claiming that
> inaccuracies in disclosure caused nonselling in a falling
> market and that unduly pessimistic predictions by the issuer
> followed by a rising market caused them to allow retro-
> spectively golden opportunities to pass.

Without the *Birnbaum* rule, the door would thus "be open to recovery
of substantial damages on the part of one who offers only his own
testimony to prove that he ever consulted a prospectus of the issuer,
that he paid any attention to it, or that the representations contained
in it damaged him." Accordingly,

> what may be called considerations of policy, which we are
> free to weigh in deciding this case, are by no means entirely
> on one side of the scale. Taken together with the prece-
> dental support for the *Birnbaum* rule over a period of more
> than 20 years, and the consistency of that rule with what we
> can glean from the intent of Congress, they lead us to con-
> clude that it is a sound rule and should be followed.

### *Twentieth Century Music Corp.* v. *Aiken*, 422 U.S. 151 (1975)

*Facts:* A fast-food shop operator (Aiken) installed four radio
speakers in the shop to enable his customers to listen to the radio.
Lacking a copyright license, he was sued for infringement of copy-
right by the American Society of Composers, Authors and Publishers
(ASCAP) on the ground that his radio received two copyrighted songs.
The broadcaster of the songs possessed a license to broadcast them.

*Question:* Does the reception of a radio broadcast of a copyrighted musical composition constitute copyright infringement, when
the copyright owner has licensed the broadcaster to perform the
composition publicly for profit?

*Decision:* No. Opinion by Justice Stewart. Vote: 7–2, Burger
and Douglas dissenting.

*Reasons:* The Copyright Act of 1909 gives to a copyright holder
a monopoly limited to specified exclusive rights in his copyrighted
works. The precise statutory issue in the present case is whether the
operator infringed the exclusive right of ASCAP under the act "[t]o

perform the copyrighted work publicly for profit." The dispositive question is whether the radio reception constituted a "performance" of the copyrighted works.

> When [the exclusive performance right] was enacted in 1909, its purpose was to prohibit unauthorized performances of copyrighted musical compositions in such public places as concert halls, theaters, restaurants, and cabarets. . . . But it was never contemplated that the members of the audience who heard the composition would themselves also be simultaneously "performing," and thus also guilty of infringement. . . .
>
> If, by analogy to a live performance in a concert hall or cabaret, a radio station "performs" a musical composition when it broadcasts it, the same analogy would seem to require the conclusion that those who listen to the broadcast through the use of radio receivers do not perform the composition.

Moreover, in *Fortnightly Corp.* v. *United Artists*, 392 U.S. 390 (1968), and *Teleprompter Corp.* v. *Columbia Broadcasting System, Inc.*, 415 U.S. 394 (1974), the Court explicitly disavowed the view that the reception of an electronic broadcast can constitute a performance when the broadcaster himself is licensed to perform the copyrighted material.

Finally,

> a ruling that a radio listener "performs" every broadcast that he receives would be highly inequitable for two distinct reasons. First, a person in Aiken's position would have no sure way of protecting himself from liability for copyright infringement except by keeping his radio set turned off.

Second, such a ruling would authorize the "sale of an untold number of licenses for what is basically a single public rendition of a copyrighted work. The exaction of such multiple tribute would go far beyond what is required for the economic protection of copyright owners, and would be wholly at odds with the balanced congressional purpose" behind the copyright protection of music: to accord the composer a fair return for his efforts while preventing the formation of oppressive monopolies.

### *Colonial Pipeline Co.* v. *Traigle,* 421 U.S. 100 (1975)

*Facts:* Louisiana imposed a corporation franchise tax on a pipeline company engaged exclusively in interstate business but qualified

119

to do business in Louisiana. The company owned 258 miles of pipe-line and several pumping stations in Louisiana that were inspected and maintained by a twenty-five-member work force. The tax purported to levy upon the corporation's privilege of enjoying in a corporate capacity the ownership or use of its capital, plant, or other property, and the use of its corporate form to do business in the state. The company brought suit to recover the franchise taxes paid on the ground that it constituted a tax on interstate commerce in violation of the commerce clause. No claim was made that the tax was discriminatory or unreasonable in light of the amount of property maintained by the company in Louisiana.

*Question:* Does Louisiana's corporate franchise tax as applied to the pipeline company violate the commerce clause?

*Decision:* No. Opinion by Justice Brennan. Vote: 7–1, Stewart dissenting. Douglas did not participate.

*Reasons:* "[T]he mere act of carrying on business in interstate commerce does not exempt a corporation from state taxation." Past decisions "have sustained nondiscriminatory, properly apportioned state corporate taxes upon foreign corporations doing an exclusively interstate business when the tax is related to a corporation's local activities and the State has provided benefits and protections for those activities for which it is justified in asking a fair and reasonable return." The challenged tax satisfies these standards. Louisiana provided the company protection of its property, access to its courts, and a corporate legal status. The tax reflected "a fairly apportioned and nondiscriminatory means of requiring [the company] to pay its just share of the cost of state government upon which [it] necessarily relies and by which it is furnished protection and benefits."

### *Allenberg Cotton Co., Inc.* v. *Pittman,* 419 U.S. 20 (1974)

*Facts:* A Tennessee cotton merchant (Allenberg) brought suit in Mississippi state court against a Mississippi farmer for breach of a contract to deliver cotton at a Mississippi warehouse. Allenberg had contracted to resell the cotton to customers outside Mississippi. The Mississippi Supreme Court held that under a Mississippi statute, Allenberg had no authority to maintain its suit because it was a foreign corporation that had not qualified to do business within the state. Allenberg contended that the Mississippi statute as applied to the facts of the case violated the commerce clause of the Constitution by interfering with the transaction of business in interstate commerce.

*Question:* Does the Mississippi statute as applied in this case violate the commerce clause?

*Decision:* Yes. Opinion by Justice Douglas. Vote: 8–1, Rehnquist dissenting.

*Reasons:* Allenberg's contract with the defendant cotton farmer is representative of a course of dealing with many other Mississippi farmers whose cotton, once sold to Allenberg, enters a long interstate pipeline that ultimately terminates at mills across the country or indeed around the world. Prior Supreme Court decisions in *Dahnke-Walker Milling Co.* v. *Bondurant*, 257 U.S. 282 (1921), *Shafer* v. *Farmers Grain Co.* 268 U.S. 189 (1925), and *H. P. Hood & Sons* v. *Du Mond*, 336 U.S. 525 (1949), make clear that the commerce clause forbids a state from restricting the right to buy or sell goods solely in interstate commerce. Because Allenberg's contracts for Mississippi cotton were made for interstate or foreign commerce, the refusal of Mississippi to enforce those contracts violates the commerce clause.

A state may require a foreign corporation doing both interstate and substantial intrastate business to obtain a license. Allenberg had minimal business contacts in Mississippi, however; it had no office, no warehouse, and no employees there. Its contracts with Mississippi farmers were arranged by an independent broker. "In short, [Allenberg's] contacts with Mississippi do not exhibit the sort of localization or intrastate character which we have required in situations where a state seeks to require a foreign corporation to qualify to do business."

### *Fry* v. *United States*, 421 U.S. 542 (1975)

*Facts:* Pursuant to the Economic Stabilization Act of 1970, the President's Pay Board ruled that Ohio state employees could receive only 7 percent of a 10.6 percent wage and salary increase authorized by state legislation. Two state employees brought suit to compel payment of the full 10.6 percent increase. They claimed that the act was not intended to include state employees and that application of the act to such employees would constitute an unconstitutional interference with state sovereign functions.

*Question:* Was the ruling of the Pay Board valid?

*Decision:* Yes. Opinion by Justice Marshall. Vote: 7–2, Douglas and Rehnquist dissenting.

121

*Reasons:* The Court pointed out:

The language and legislative history of the Act leave no doubt that Congress intended that it apply to employees throughout the economy, including those employed by state and local governments. . . . Indeed, in framing the Act, Congress specifically rejected an amendment that would have exempted employees of state and local governments. . . . The only remaining question is whether it could do so consistent with the constitutional limitations on its power.

The claim that application of the act unconstitutionally intrudes upon state sovereignty is foreclosed by *Maryland* v. *Wirtz*, 392 U.S. 183 (1968). There the Court held that the minimum wage and overtime provisions of the Fair Labor Standards Act could be constitutionally applied to state-operated schools and hospitals. "*Wirtz* reiterated the principle that States are not immune from all federal regulation under the Commerce Clause merely because of their sovereign status." The Pay Board ruling at issue is less intrusive on state sovereignty than the intrusion involved in *Wirtz*.

In addition,

Congress enacted the Economic Stabilization Act as an emergency measure to counter severe inflation that threatened the national economy. The method it chose, under the Commerce Clause, was to give the President authority to freeze virtually all wages and prices, including the wages of state and local government employees. In 1971, when the freeze was activated, state and local government employees composed 14 percent of the Nation's work force. It seems inescapable that the effectiveness of federal action would have been drastically impaired if wage increases to this sizeable group of employees were left outside the reach of these emergency federal wage controls.

## United States v. Reliable Transfer Co., Inc., 421 U.S. 397 (1975)

*Facts:* A coastal tanker brought suit in federal district court seeking to recover damages against the United States. It claimed it was stranded because of the failure of the Coast Guard to maintain a breakwater light. The district court found that the vessel's grounding was caused 25 percent by the Coast Guard's failure and 75 percent by its own fault. However, it held that the settled admiralty rule of divided damages required that each party bear one-half of the damages to the vessel.

*Question:* Should the admiralty rule of divided damages be replaced by a rule generally allocating damages among parties proportionate to their comparative degree of fault?

*Decision:* Yes. Opinion by Justice Stewart. Vote: 9–0.

*Reasons:* The Court stated:

> More than a century ago, in *The Schooner Catherine* v. *Dickinson*, 58 U.S. (17 How.) 170, this Court established in our admiralty law the rule of divided damages. That rule, most commonly applied in cases of collision between two vessels, requires the equal division of property damage whenever both parties are found to be guilty of contributing fault, whatever the relative degree of their fault may have been. The courts of every major maritime nation except ours have long since abandoned that rule, and now assess damages in such cases on the basis of proportionate fault when such an allocation can reasonably be made.

The original justification for the rule of divided damages was that it provided "a means of apportioning damages where it was difficult to measure which party was more at fault." That justification, however, does not warrant application of the rule "where an allocation of disparate proportional fault has been made. Potential problems of proof in some cases hardly require adherence to an archaic and unfair rule in all cases."

> We hold that when two or more parties have contributed by their fault to cause property damage in a maritime collision or stranding, liability for such damages is to be allocated among the parties proportionately to the comparative degree of their fault, and that liability for such damages is to be allocated equally only when the parties are equally at fault or when it is not possible fairly to measure the comparative degree of their fault.

## United Housing Foundation, Inc. v. Forman, 421 U.S. 837 (1975)

*Facts:* Residents of a large nonprofit cooperative housing project, subsidized by New York state, brought suit against the developer and others under the Securities Act of 1933 and the Securities Exchange Act of 1934 (Securities Acts). The residents were required to purchase stock in the housing cooperative corporation for $25 as a condition of acquiring an apartment. The stock was generally nontransferable and had no voting rights. It was required that it be offered to the cooperative corporation at $25 by any tenant who wanted to terminate his occupancy. The theory of the suit was that the defendants had misrepresented the probable monthly rental charges to the residents in connection with the sale of the cooperative stock. A federal district court dismissed the claims on the ground that the stock was not a "security" within the protection of the Securities Acts.

*Question:* Was the cooperative stock a "security" for purposes of the Securities Acts?

*Decision:* No. Opinion by Justice Powell. Vote: 6–3, Brennan, Douglas, and White dissenting.

*Reasons:* The Securities Acts define "security" in broad and general terms to include the many types of instruments that in our commercial world fall within the ordinary concept of a security. In *SEC v. C. M. Joiner Leasing Corp.,* 320 U.S. 344 (1943), and *SEC v. W. J. Howey Co.,* 328 U.S. 293 (1946), the Court established the general principle that a security is

> an investment in a common venture premised on a reasonable expectation of profits to be derived from the entreprenurial or managerial efforts of others. By profits, the Court has meant either capital appreciation resulting from the development of the initial investment . . . or a participation in earnings resulting from the use of investors' funds. . . . In such cases the investor is "attracted solely by the prospects of a return" on his investment.

Here, in contrast, the cooperative residents purchased their stock solely by the prospect of acquiring a place to live and not for financial returns on their investments. In addition, the allegedly misleading statement of the defendants nowhere seeks to attract investors by the promise of profits resulting from the efforts of promoters or third parties.

It is claimed, nevertheless, that the stock held the promise of "profits" in three ways: tax deductions for monthly interest payments on the cooperative mortgage, low rentals, and rental rebates through income earned in the operation of commercial facilities within the housing project. Tax deductions or low rents made possible by a government subsidy, however, do not constitute profits under any appropriate theory. And the commercial facilities in question were

> established not as a means of returning profits to tenants, but for the purpose of making essential services available

for the residents of this enormous complex. . . . Undoubtedly they make [the cooperative] a more attractive housing opportunity, but the possibility of some rental reduction is not an "expectation of profit" in the sense found necessary in *Howey.*

It is also claimed that the cooperative stock is a security because the statutory definition of that term includes the words "any . . . stock." However, "[b]ecause securities transactions are economic in character Congress intended the application of these statutes to turn on the economic realities underlying a transaction, and not on the name appended thereto."

## *Regional Rail Reorganization Act Cases,* 419 U.S. 102 (1974)[42]

*Facts:* Congress enacted the Regional Rail Reorganization Act of 1973 (Rail Act) to assist in the reorganization of several bankrupt northeast and midwest railroads. The Rail Act established a United States Railway Association (USRA) to prepare a plan for reorganizing the bankrupt railroads through the transfer of designated rail properties to a private corporation (Conrail). In exchange for their property, the railroads are to receive securities of Conrail, plus up to $500 million in USRA obligations guaranteed by the United States. USRA must submit its reorganization plan to Congress by July 26, 1975, and it becomes effective if neither house of Congress disapproves it within sixty days.

Within ninety days after approval, the plan must be submitted to a special court which determines whether the transfer and conveyance of property is fair and equitable to the estate of each railroad. If it finds that the transfer is not fair and equitable, the special court may order the issuance of additional Conrail securities and USRA obligations (subject to the overall $500 million limitation).

Until the USRA plan becomes effective, none of the railroads covered by the Rail Act may discontinue service or abandon any railroad line without USRA approval.

Investors of the Penn Central Transportation Company brought suit challenging the constitutionality of the Rail Act on the ground that in two respects it effects a taking of rail properties without just compensation in violation of the Fifth Amendment. They contended

---

[42] This decision may also be located under the following case names: Blanchette v. Connecticut General Insurance Corp., Smith v. United States, U.S. Railway Assn. v. Connecticut General Insurance Corp., and United States v. Connecticut General Insurance Corp.

that the Conrail securities and USRA obligations would not be con-stitutionally sufficient compensation for the rail properties transferred and that the severe inhibitions imposed on discontinuing unprofitable service and rail lines would constitute an unconstitutional erosion of the estate of Penn Central before the USRA plan was approved.

*Question:* Does the Rail Act violate the Fifth Amendment pro-hibition against the taking of property without payment of just compensation?

*Decision:* No. Opinion by Justice Brennan. Vote: 7–2, Douglas and Stewart dissenting.

*Reasons:* The determinative issues in this case are whether the railroads may sue in the Court of Claims under the Tucker Act, 28 U.S.C. 1491, to recover any deficiency of constitutional dimension in the compensation provided under the Rail Act, and if so, whether that remedy is constitutionally adequate.

The Tucker Act provides in relevant part that "the Court of Claims shall have jurisdiction to render judgment upon any claim against the United States founded . . . upon the Constitution." A claim based upon a taking of property under the Fifth Amendment plainly falls within the literal words of the act. It is argued, however, that jurisdiction under the Tucker Act was withdrawn with respect to constitutional claims involving the Rail Act. Accepted canons of statutory construction compel rejection of that argument.

The Rail Act itself is silent on the issue of Tucker Act jurisdic-tion. Its legislative history is ambiguous on the question. Canons of statutory construction teach that repeals by implication are disfavored and that ambiguities should be resolved in favor of a constitutional interpretation. Accordingly, the Tucker Act remedy is available to provide just compensation for any taking which occurs under the Rail Act.

It is claimed, nevertheless, that the Tucker Act is inadequate because the taking of railroad properties is an exercise of the power of eminent domain requiring full payment in cash. Part of the pay-ment under the Rail Act would be Conrail securities and USRA obligations. This claim fails for two reasons. First, the Court has never held that "compensation other than money is an inadequate form of compensation under eminent domain statutes." Second, the Rail Act is valid as a reorganization statute and is not an exercise of the government's power of eminent domain.

Finally, the Court rejected the contention that because the Rail Act applied only to bankrupt railroads in a certain region of the country, it violated Article I, section 8, clause 4, of the Constitution which requires federal bankruptcy laws to be "uniform . . . throughout the United States." It reasoned that "the uniformity provision does not deny Congress power to take into account differences that exist between different parts of the country, and to fashion legislation to resolve geographically isolated problems."

## Freedom of Information

Enacted in 1966 to make public access to government records easier, the Freedom of Information Act promises to spawn an increasing number of federal lawsuits. Generally speaking, the act requires an agency to disclose any "identifiable record" unless it falls within any of nine enumerated exempt categories. In 1974, Congress amended the act [43] to narrow some of the exempt categories, overrule the Supreme Court's interpretation of the national security exemption in *Environmental Protection Agency* v. *Mink*, 410 U.S. 73 (1973), require agencies to respond to requests for information within strict time limits, reduce the permissible charges for obtaining information, and authorize an award of attorneys' fees in suits brought to compel disclosure of information. These amendments are likely to encourage more lawsuits under the act. In practice, numerous requests for information come from corporations that perceive a business use for the information they seek.

The three significant Freedom of Information Act cases of the Court this term established the following principles:

—Exemption 3, which protects materials "specifically exempted from disclosure by statute" includes all statutes permitting the confidentiality of information.

—Exemption 5, which generally protects intra-agency communications includes communications made before a final agency decision on a subject but not the postdecisional communications designed to explain it.

—Exemption 5 protects intra-agency memoranda which direct the filing of a complaint for adjudication by that agency.

—An agency memorandum reflecting an unreviewable decision not to file a complaint constitutes a final agency decision which must be disclosed.

---

[43] 88 Stat. 1561 (1974).

## *NLRB* v. *Sears, Roebuck & Co.*, 421 U.S. 132 (1975)

*Facts:* Pursuant to the Freedom of Information Act, 5 U.S.C. 552, Sears, Roebuck & Co. (Sears) sought disclosure of certain memoranda, known as advice memoranda and appeals memoranda, and related documents generated by the Office of the General Counsel of the National Labor Relations Board in the course of deciding whether or not to permit the filing with the board of complaints of unfair labor practices. Generally speaking, the act requires an agency to disclose upon request any "identifiable record" unless it falls within any of nine enumerated exempt categories listed in section 552(b). The act also requires agency disclosure of "final opinions . . . made in the adjudication of cases," and "instructions to staff that affect a member of the public."

Sears claimed that the memoranda were disclosable either because they were unprotected by any exemption or because they constituted final opinions and instructions to staff that affect a member of the public. In refusing disclosure, the general counsel asserted that the memoranda were not final opinions and were protected as intra-agency communications under section 552(b)(5) (exemption 5).

*Question:* Were the requested memoranda protected from disclosure under the act?

*Decision:* The memoranda explaining decisions not to file a complaint are disclosable, but those explaining why a complaint was filed are protected. Opinion by Justice White. Vote: 8–0. Powell did not participate.

*Reasons:* Under the National Labor Relations Act, the general counsel has unreviewable authority to determine whether a complaint of unfair labor practice shall be filed with the board. In making that determination the general counsel prepares a memorandum explaining the legal or factual basis for the decision. When the general counsel determines not to file a complaint, the memorandum constitutes a final agency decision which must be disclosed.

That conclusion does not undermine the purpose of exemption 5. That exemption protects only those documents that an agency would be privileged to withhold from a party in civil litigation. The privileges relevant to this case are the privilege for confidential intra-agency advisory opinions and the attorney-client and attorney work-product privileges. The first privilege is designed

> to prevent injury to the quality of agency decisions. The quality of a particular agency decision will clearly be

affected by the communications received by the decision-maker on the subject of the decision prior to the time the decision is made. However, it is difficult to see how the quality of a decision will be affected by communications with respect to the decision occurring after the decision is finally reached; and therefore equally difficult to see how the quality of the decision will be affected by forced disclosure of such communications, as long as prior communications and the ingredients of the decisionmaking process are not disclosed.

Accordingly, exemption 5 protects predecisional communications but not communications made after the decision and designed to explain it.

The attorney work-product privilege covers memoranda "prepared by an attorney in contemplation of litigation which set forth the attorney's theory of the case and his litigation strategy." That privilege clearly is unavailable to protect memoranda which explain why litigation was not commenced.

Exemption 5, however, does protect memoranda which direct the filing of a complaint of unfair labor practice. Such memoranda, prepared in contemplation of the upcoming litigation, will contain the general counsel's theory of the case and perhaps litigation strategy. The attorney work-product privilege clearly applies to these documents. In addition, the documents are not disclosable final opinions made in the adjudication of cases because they merely authorize litigation before the board.

The Court rejected the contention of the general counsel that documents incorporated by reference in disclosable advice and appeals memoranda may remain protected under exemption 5 as intra-agency memoranda. The Court reasoned that

> [t]he probability that an agency employee will be inhibited from freely advising a decisionmaker for fear that his advice, *if adopted*, will become public is slight. First, when adopted, the reasoning becomes that of the agency and becomes *its* responsibility to defend. Second, agency employees will generally be encouraged rather than discouraged by public knowledge that their policy suggestions have been adopted by the agency. (Emphasis in original.)

Accordingly, the Court held that

> if an agency chooses *expressly* to adopt or incorporate by reference an intra-agency memorandum previously covered by Exemption 5 in what would otherwise be a final opinion, that memorandum may be withheld only on the ground that

it falls within the coverage of some exemption other than Exemption 5. (Emphasis in original.)

The Court added, however, that documents incorporated by reference in disclosable advice and appeals memoranda which were previously protected by exemption 7 did not lose their exempt status by reason of incorporation. That exemption, generally speaking, protects investigatory files compiled for purposes of law enforcement if their disclosure would cause some particular harm to law enforcement or to individuals.

## *Renegotiation Board* v. *Grumman Aircraft Engineering Corp.*, 421 U.S. 168 (1975)

*Facts:* The five-member Renegotiation Board, pursuant to the Renegotiation Act of 1951, has the duty of determining whether certain government contractors have earned, and must refund, "excess profits" on their government contracts. In making those determinations, the board frequently receives advisory reports from its regional boards and from a division of the board usually consisting of three members. Suit was brought under the Freedom of Information Act, 5 U.S.C. 552, seeking disclosure of the advisory reports on the grounds that they were "final opinions" of the board under section 552(a)(2)(A) and unprotected by any of the nine exempt categories of information specified in section 552(b). (See *NLRB* v. *Sears, Roebuck & Co.*, 421 U.S. 132 [1975], for a discussion of the basic statutory provisions of the act.) In refusing disclosure, the board contended that the reports were not final opinions and were protected under exemption 5 as "inter-agency or intra-agency memoranda . . . which would not be available by law to a party other than an agency in litigation with the agency."

*Question:* Are the requested advisory reports to the board protected from disclosure under exemption 5?

*Decision:* Yes. Opinion by Justice White. Vote: 7–1, Douglas dissenting. Powell did not participate.

*Reasons:* In *NLRB* v. *Sears, Roebuck & Co.*, the Court held that

exemption 5 incorporates the privileges which the Government enjoys under the relevant statutory and case law in the pretrial discovery context; and both Exemption 5 and the case law which it incorporates distinguish between predecisional memoranda prepared in order to assist an agency decision-maker in arriving at his decision, which are exempt from disclosure, and post-decisional memoranda setting forth the reasons for an agency decision already made, which are not. Because only the full Board has the power by law to make the decision whether excessive profits exist; because both types of reports involved in this case are prepared prior to that decision and are used by the Board in its deliberations; and because the evidence utterly fails to support the conclusion that the reasoning in the Reports is adopted by the Board as *its* reasoning, even when it agrees with the conclusion of a Report, we conclude that the Reports are not final opinions and do fall within Exemption 5.

It follows from the *Sears* rule that the Renegotiation Board's advisory reports are protected from disclosure as predecisional memoranda.

## *Administrator, Federal Aviation Administration* v. *Robertson*, 422 U.S. 255 (1975)

*Facts:* A public-interest group sought disclosure under the Freedom of Information Act of Federal Aviation Administration (FAA) reports analyzing the operation and maintenance performance of commercial airlines. The FAA refused disclosure on the ground, *inter alia*, that the reports were protected under exemption 3 of the act, 5 U.S.C. 552(b)(3). Exemption 3 permits withholding of materials "specifically exempted from disclosure by statute." The FAA claimed that section 1104 of the Federal Aviation Act exempted the requested reports from disclosure. That section authorizes the FAA to withhold information upon the request of an interested person if it determines that disclosure "would adversely affect the interests of such person . . . and is not required in the interests of the public." The Air Transport Association had requested the FAA to withhold the reports at issue.

*Question:* Were the FAA reports exempt from disclosure under exemption 3 of the act?

*Decision:* Yes. Opinion by Chief Justice Burger. Vote: 7–2, Brennan and Douglas dissenting.

*Reasons:* The language of exemption 3 provides no clear standard for determining when a statute falls within its coverage. Its legislative history, however, reveals that Congress in passing the act was aware of the necessity to deal expressly with inconsistent laws. There is clear evidence that exemption 3 was intended to preserve unmodified numerous statutes which restricted public access to specific government records. This fact, together with the general rule of statutory construction disfavoring repeals by implication, compel the conclusion that exemption 3 covers all statutes permitting the confidentiality of information.

## Government Benefits: Welfare and Social Security

As the number of persons receiving funds from the welfare and social security programs of the federal government increases, the decisions of the Court interpreting various statutes applicable to these programs and determining their constitutionality acquire greater fiscal significance. In fiscal 1975, approximately 31 million persons received $63.5 billion in social security benefits, and in fiscal year 1974 approximately 10.8 million individuals received $8 billion in welfare under the Aid to Families with Dependent Children program.

In establishing important constitutional doctrine, the Court in *Weinberger* v. *Salfi*, 422 U.S. 749, rejected an attack on social security provisions that denied insurance benefits to the widows and stepchildren of a deceased wage earner if their respective relationships commenced less than nine months before the wage earner's death. In applying a lenient standard to judge the constitutionality of the challenged provisions, the Court indicated that statutory classifications embodied in government benefit programs pass constitutional muster unless wholly irrational.

In two decisions interpreting provisions of the Aid to Families with Dependent Children program, the Court ruled in *Burns* v. *Alcala*, 420 U.S. 575, that pregnant women are not entitled to collect welfare benefits for their unborn children and, in *Philbrook* v. *Glodgett*, 421 U.S. 707, that welfare payments may not be denied to families who decline unemployment compensation of a lesser amount.

## *Burns* v. *Alcala*, 420 U.S. 575 (1975)

*Facts:* The state of Iowa denied pregnant women welfare under the federally assisted program of Aid to Families with Dependent Children (AFDC) on the theory that they had no "dependent children." The women brought suit contending, *inter alia*, that the Iowa policy of denying AFDC benefits to unborn children violated section 602(a)(10) of the Social Security Act. That section requires all states that participate in the AFDC program to offer benefits to all persons eligible under the federal definition of "dependent child" in section 606(a) of the act. That term is defined as "a needy child (1) who has been deprived of parental support or care by reason of the death, continued absence from the home, or physical or mental incapacity of a parent, and who is living with his father, mother," or certain other designated relatives, and (2) who is under the age of eighteen, or under the age of twenty-one and a student. The women claimed that section 606(a) should be interpreted to include unborn children.

*Question:* Must states receiving federal financial aid under the AFDC program offer welfare benefits to pregnant women on behalf of their unborn children?

*Decision:* No. Opinion by Justice Powell. Vote: 7–1, Marshall dissenting. Douglas did not participate.

*Reasons:* The ordinary meaning of *child* and the statutory context of *dependent child* compel the conclusion that Congress did not intend to cover unborn children in the AFDC program. As originally enacted, the Social Security Act provided benefits only to certain "living" children. "The failure [of the Act] to provide explicitly for the special circumstances of pregnant women strongly suggests that Congress had no thought of providing AFDC benefits to 'dependent children' before birth."

The original purposes of the AFDC program also supports this conclusion. It was "to substitute for the practice of removing needy children from their homes and placing them in institutions, and to free widowed and divorced mothers from the necessity of working, so that they could remain home to supervise their children."

### *Philbrook v. Glodgett,* 421 U.S. 707 (1975)

*Facts:* Under the federally assisted Aid to Families with Dependent Children (AFDC) program, a participating state may receive federal funding for the payment of welfare benefits to children with unemployed fathers. Under section 407(b)(2)(C)(ii) of the Social Security Act, however, a child can be excluded from the unemployed-father program only if his father "receives unemployment compensation." Vermont promulgated a regulation which disqualified children from its unemployed-father program if the father was eligible for unemployment compensation. Vermont families that would receive more in AFDC benefits than their fathers would receive in unemployment compensation challenged the constitutionality of the Vermont regulation on the ground that it conflicted with section 407(b)(2)(C)(ii) of the act.

*Question:* Does the Vermont welfare regulation impermissibly conflict with the act?

*Decision:* Yes. Opinion by Justice Rehnquist. Vote: 9–0.

*Reasons:* Section 407(b)(2)(C)(ii) speaks in terms of a "father [who] *receives* unemployment compensation" rather than a "father [who] is *eligible* to receive unemployment compensation." (Court's emphasis.) Neither the legislative history of that section nor the structure of the act provides cogent evidence that when Congress used the term *receives* it intended to include within that term persons who were only eligible to receive unemployment compensation. Accordingly, "it is apparent that the Vermont definition of 'unemployed father,' which has been applied to exclude unemployed fathers who are eligible for unemployment compensation, conflicts with section 407(b)(2)(C)(ii)." Vermont must provide welfare to children with such fathers if it wishes to receive federal funding for its unemployed-father program.

## *Weinberger* v. *Salfi,* 422 U.S. 749 (1975)

*Facts:* A widow and stepchild of a deceased wage earner were denied social security insurance benefits under 42 U.S.C. 416(c)(5) and (e)(2), on the ground that they commenced their respective relationships to the wage earner less than nine months before his death. They successfully challenged the constitutionality of the nine-month duration-of-relationship requirements of those sections in federal district court. That court held that the sections created an unconstitutional irrebuttable presumption that marriages preceding a wage earner's death by less than nine months were fraudulently entered into for the purpose of obtaining social security benefits.

*Question:* Are sections 416(c)(5) and (e)(2) unconstitutional?

*Decision:* No. Opinion by Justice Rehnquist. Vote: 6–3, Douglas, Brennan, and Marshall dissenting.

*Reasons:* A classification created under the social security statutes is constitutionally permissible if it has any rational basis. The challenged duration-of-relationship requirements were established to prevent the payment of social security insurance benefits to individuals who married for the sole purpose of acquiring such benefits. When measured against its purpose the nine-month requirement operates imprecisely. Some whose sham marriages last nine months may receive social security benefits, whereas others whose legitimate marriages lasted a shorter time are barred. But imprecision is not the test of constitutionality. Rather, the test is

> whether Congress, its concern having been reasonably aroused by the possibility of an abuse which it legitimately desired to avoid, could rationally have concluded both that a particular limitation or qualification would protect against its occurrence, and that the expense and other difficulties of individual determinations justified the inherent imprecision of a prophylactic rule.

The duration-of-relationship requirement reflects a legitimate congressional concern over the integrity of both the Social Security Trust Fund and the marriage relationship. It clearly operates "to lessen the likelihood of abuse through sham relationships entered in contemplation of imminent death. . . . Congress could rationally have concluded that any imprecision from which it might suffer was justified by its ease and certainty of operation."

## Miscellaneous: Aliens, Impoundment, Coastal Lands

Farm-worker unions suffered a defeat in *Saxbe* v. *Bustos*, 419 U.S. 65, when the Court upheld a longstanding Immigration and Naturalization Service practice of permitting aliens who reside in Mexico and Canada to commute daily or seasonally to work in the United States. The Court noted that a contrary conclusion might produce unpredictable economic and international consequences.

Municipalities prevailed in the first so-called impoundment decision of the Court, which stemmed from President Nixon's refusal to allot sums to construct sewage treatment plants under the Water Pollution Control Act. The government did not claim that the President has a constitutional right to impound appropriated funds. Instead, it argued that the Pollution Control Act conferred discretion upon the President to allot less than the maximum amount of authorized funds. A unanimous Court rejected that claim in *Train* v. *City of New York*, 420 U.S. 35.

The increased price of oil and concern over oil pollution and oil refineries led to a suit between the United States and the thirteen states bordering on the Atlantic Ocean. The states claimed sovereign rights over the seabed and subsoil underlying the ocean and located more than three miles from the coast. These claims were advanced shortly before the United States planned to lease drilling rights to oil companies in part of that area. A unanimous Court, in *United States* v. *Maine*, 420 U.S. 515, ruled that the United States government possesses paramount rights over the seas as an attribute of its jurisdiction over foreign commerce, foreign affairs, and national defense.

### *Saxbe* v. *Bustos*, 419 U.S. 65 (1974)

*Facts:* The Immigration and Naturalization Service (INS) permits aliens who reside in Canada and Mexico to commute daily or seasonally to work in the United States. Under federal immigration laws, such an alien is authorized to enter the United States only if he is "lawfully admitted for permanent residence [in the United States]" and "is returning from a temporary visit abroad." Certain farmers and a union of farm workers brought suit seeking to enjoin the INS practice of permitting aliens to commute to work in the United States. They claimed that since these aliens resided permanently outside the United States, they were not "returning from a temporary visit abroad" within the meaning of the immigration laws when they commuted to work in the United States.

*Question:* Is the INS practice of permitting aliens who reside in Canada and Mexico to commute to work in the United States authorized under federal immigration laws?

*Decision:* Yes. Opinion by Justice Douglas. Vote: 5–4, White, Brennan, Marshall, and Blackmun dissenting.

*Reasons:* The challenged INS practice is supported both by the wording and legislative history of the immigration statutes and a long history of their administrative construction. The aliens participating in the commuter program had been lawfully accorded the privilege of residing permanently in the United States. They were thus "lawfully admitted for permanent residence," although they did not actually reside in the United States. Longstanding administrative construction, unchanged by Congress, compels the conclusion that the aliens can be viewed as "returning from a temporary visit abroad" when they commute to work in the United States. Any change in this construction would "implicate so many policies and raise so many problems of a political, economic, and social nature that it is fit that the judiciary recuse itself."

## *Train* v. *City of New York*, 420 U.S. 35 (1975)

*Facts:* Under the Federal Water Pollution Control Act Amendments of 1972, the federal government subsidizes 75 percent of the cost of municipal sewers and sewage treatment works. Under section 207, $5 billion in fiscal 1973 and $6 billion in fiscal 1974 is authorized to be appropriated for these purposes. Section 205(a) provides that the amounts authorized under section 207 "shall be allotted by the Administrator [of the Environmental Protection Agency] not later than the January 1st immediately preceding the fiscal year for which authorized." Pursuant to the direction of President Nixon, however, the administrator determined not to allot the maximum amounts provided under section 207, but instead to allot for fiscal 1973 and 1974 sums not to exceed $2 billion and $3 billion respectively. New York City and other municipalities brought suit seeking a declaration that the administrator was required to allot to the states the full amounts authorized under section 207.

*Question:* Does the act require the administrator to allot the full sums authorized to be appropriated in section 207?

*Decision:* Yes. Opinion by Justice White. Vote: 9–0.

*Reasons:* Section 205(a) literally directs the administrator to allot to the states the amounts authorized under section 207. The legislative history of the act does not argue persuasively for a different interpretation. The act "was intended to provide a firm commitment of substantial sums within a relatively limited period of time in an effort to achieve an early solution of what was deemed an urgent problem." Even assuming that Congress intended to grant the executive some sort of control over outlays under the act, its legislative history clearly indicates that it "was to be exercised at the point where funds were obligated and not in connection with the threshold functions of alloting funds to the States." (Under the act, funds are obligated when the administrator approves a state application for a municipal sewer or sewage treatment project.)

## *United States* v. *Maine*, 420 U.S. 515 (1975)

*Facts:* The United States brought suit against the thirteen states bordering on the Atlantic Ocean seeking a declaration that it possessed exclusive sovereign rights over the seabed and subsoil underlying the Atlantic Ocean and located more than three miles from the coast. The states claimed proprietary rights in the seabed as successors in title to certain grantees of the crown of England.

*Question:* Does the United States possess paramount sovereign rights over the disputed Atlantic seabed and subsoil?

*Decision:* Yes. Opinion by Justice White. Vote: 8–0. Douglas did not participate.

*Reasons:* In *United States* v. *California,* 332 U.S. 19 (1947), the Court sustained the claim of the United States to ownership of the seabed underlying the Pacific Ocean and extending three miles from the California coast. California claimed ownership to the seabed on the theory that the original thirteen states acquired from the English crown title to the seabed within three miles of the Atlantic coast and that since California was admitted as a state on an "equal footing" with the original states, it had title to a similar three-mile strip underlying the Pacific Ocean. The Court rejected that claim, holding that protection and control of the sea is a function of national external sovereignty, "and that in our constitutional system paramount rights over the ocean waters and their seabeds were vested in the Federal Government." The *California* decision and others unmistakably stand for the constitutional principle that the federal government, as an attribute of its jurisdiction over foreign commerce, foreign affairs and national defense, has paramount rights over the seas. "To reexamine the constitutional underpinnings of the *California* case and of those cases which followed and explicated the rule that paramount rights to the offshore seabed inhere in the Federal Government as an incident of national sovereignty" would be inappropriate.

> [I]n the almost 30 years since *California,* a great deal of public and private business has been transacted in accordance with those decisions and in accordance with major legislation enacted by Congress, a principal purpose of which was to resolve the "interminable litigation" arising over the controversy of the ownership of the lands underlying the marginal sea. . . . Both the Submerged Lands Act and the Outer Continental Shelf Lands Act which soon followed proceeded from the premises established by prior Court decisions and provided for the orderly development of offshore resources.

This major legislation and the commercial activity which followed it should not be disturbed at this late date by calling into question the constitutional premise of the *California* decision.

# INDEX OF CASES

Administrator, Federal Aviation Administration v. Robertson,
422 U.S. 255 .......................................... 131

Albemarle Paper Co. v. Moody, 422 U.S. 405 ................... 66

Allenberg Cotton Co., Inc. v. Pittman, 419 U.S. 20 .............. 120

Alyeska Pipeline Service Co. v. The Wilderness Society, 421 U.S. 240 . 91

Austin v. New Hampshire, 420 U.S. 656 ....................... 65

Bigelow v. Virginia, 421 U.S. 809 ............................ 51

Blanchette v. Connecticut General Insurance Corp., 419 U.S. 102 ..... 125

Blue Chip Stamps v. Manor Drug Stores, 427 U.S. 723 ............. 116

Breed v. Jones, 421 U.S. 519 ................................ 23

Brown v. Illinois, 422 U.S. 590 .............................. 17

Burns v. Alcala, 420 U.S. 575 ............................... 132

Cantrell v. Forest City Publishing Co., 419 U.S. 245 .............. 68

Chapman v. Meier, 420 U.S. 1 ............................... 72

City of Richmond v. United States, 422 U.S. 358 ................. 76

Colonial Pipeline Co. v. Traigle, 421 U.S. 100 ................... 119

Connell Construction Co., Inc. v. Plumbers and Steamfitters,
Local No. 100, 421 U.S. 616 .............................. 106

Cort v. Ash, 422 U.S. 66 ................................... 75

Cousins v. Wigoda, 419 U.S. 477 ............................ 71

Cox Broadcasting Corp. v. Cohn, 420 U.S. 469 .................. 50

Eastland v. U.S. Servicemen's Fund, 421 U.S. 491 ................ 59

Emporium Capwell Co. v. Western Addition Community Organization,
420 U.S. 50 ............................................ 112

Erznoznik v. City of Jacksonville, 422 U.S. 205 .................. 61

Faretta v. California, 422 U.S. 806 ........................... 25

Fry v. United States, 421 U.S. 542 ........................... 121

Gerstein v. Pugh, 420 U.S. 103 .............................. 30

Goldfarb v. Virginia State Bar, 421 U.S. 773 ..................... 108
Gonzalez v. Automatic Employees Credit Union, 419 U.S. 90 ........ 88
Goss v. Lopez, 419 U.S. 565 .................................... 43
Herring v. New York, 422 U.S. 853 ............................. 26
Hicks v. Miranda, 422 U.S. 332 ................................ 81
Hill v. Stone, 421 U.S. 289 .................................... 74
Huffman v. Pursue, Ltd., 420 U.S. 592 .......................... 83
Jackson v. Metropolitan Edison Co., 419 U.S. 345 ................. 54
Johnson v. Mississippi, 421 U.S. 213 ........................... 92
Kugler v. Helfant, 421 U.S. 117 ............................... 84
Maness v. Meyers, 419 U.S. 449 ............................... 18
Meek v. Pittenger, 421 U.S. 349 ............................... 41
MTM, Inc. v. Baxley, 420 U.S. 799 ............................ 87
Mullaney v. Wilbur, 421 U.S. 684 ............................. 32
Muniz v. Hoffman, 422 U.S. 454 .............................. 114
Murphy v. Florida, 421 U.S. 794 .............................. 34
NLRB v. J. Weingarten, Inc., 420 U.S. 251 ...................... 111
NLRB v. Sears, Roebuck & Co., 421 U.S. 132 ................... 128
North Georgia Finishing, Inc. v. Di-Chem, Inc., 419 U.S. 601 ........ 58
O'Connor v. Donaldson, 422 U.S. 563 .......................... 53
Oregon v. Hass, 420 U.S. 714 ................................. 16
Philbrook v. Glodgett, 421 U.S. 707 ........................... 133
Regional Rail Reorganization Act Cases, 419 U.S. 102 .............. 125
Renegotiation Board v. Grumman Aircraft Engineering Corp.,
     421 U.S. 168 ............................................ 130
Saxbe v. Bustos, 419 U.S. 65 .................................. 136
Schick v. Reed, 419 U.S. 256 .................................. 38
Schlesinger v. Ballard, 419 U.S. 498 ........................... 98
Schlesinger v. Councilman, 420 U.S. 738 ........................ 85
Serfass v. United States, 420 U.S. 377 .......................... 22
Smith v. United States, 419 U.S. 102 ........................... 125
Sosna v. Iowa, 419 U.S. 393 ................................... 55
Southeastern Promotions, Ltd v. Conrad, 420 U.S. 546 ............. 62
Stanton v. Stanton, 421 U.S. 7 ................................ 99
Taylor v. Louisiana, 419 U.S. 522 ............................. 95
Train v. City of New York, 420 U.S. 35 ........................ 137
Twentieth Century Music Corp. v. Aiken, 422 U.S. 151 ............ 118
United Housing Foundation, Inc. v. Forman, 421 U.S. 837 ........... 123
United States v. American Building Maintenance Industries,
     422 U.S. 271 ............................................ 110
United States v. Bisceglia, 420 U.S. 141 ........................ 32
United States v. Brignoni-Ponce, 422 U.S. 873 ................... 28

United States v. Citizens and Southern National Bank, 422 U.S. 86 .... 103
United States v. Connecticut General Insurance Corp., 419 U.S. 102 ... 125
United States v. Jenkins, 420 U.S. 358 .......................... 21
United States v. Maine, 420 U.S. 515 .......................... 137
United States v. National Assn. of Securities Dealers, Inc., 422 U.S. 694 102
United States v. Nobles, 422 U.S. 225 .......................... 35
United States v. Ortiz, 422 U.S. 891 .......................... 27
United States v. Park, 421 U.S. 658 .......................... 36
United States v. Peltier, 422 U.S. 531 .......................... 26
United States v. Reliable Transfer Co., Inc., 421 U.S. 397 ........... 122
United States v. Wilson, 420 U.S. 332 .......................... 20
U.S. Railway Assn. v. Connecticut General Insurance Corp.,
    419 U.S. 102 .......................... 125
Warth v. Seldin, 422 U.S. 490 .......................... 89
Weinberger v. Salfi, 422 U.S. 749 .......................... 134
Weinberger v. Wiesenfeld, 420 U.S. 636 .......................... 97
Withrow v. Larkin, 421 U.S. 35 .......................... 63
Wood v. Strickland, 420 U.S. 308 .......................... 45

# SUBJECT INDEX

Abortion
  Bigelow v. Virginia, 51
Abstention
  Hicks v. Miranda, 81
  Huffman v. Pursue, Ltd., 83
  Kugler v. Helfant, 84
  Schlesinger v. Councilman, 85
Access to courts
  Sosna v. Iowa, 55
Access to state courts
  Allenberg Cotton Co., Inc. v. Pittman, 120
Admiralty law
  United States v. Reliable Transfer Co., Inc., 122
Advertisements
  Bigelow v. Virginia, 51
Aid to Families with Dependent Children
  Burns v. Alcala, 132
  Philbrook v. Glodgett, 133
Aliens
  Saxbe v. Bustos, 136
  United States v. Brignoni-Ponce, 28
American Society of Composers, Authors and Publishers
  Twentieth Century Music Corp. v. Aiken, 118
Annexations
  City of Richmond v. United States, 76
Antitrust
  United States v. American Building Maintenance Industries, 110
Antitrust exemptions
  Connell Construction Co., Inc. v. Plumbers and Steamfitters, Local No. 100, 106
  Goldfarb v. Virginia State Bar, 108

Antitrust immunity
  United States v. Citizens and Southern National Bank, 103
  United States v. National Assn. of Securities Dealers, Inc., 102
Appellate jurisdiction of the Supreme Court
  Gonzalez v. Automatic Employees Credit Union, 88
  Hicks v. Miranda, 81
  MTM, Inc. v. Baxley, 87
Armed forces
  Schlesinger v. Ballard, 98
Attorneys
  Maness v. Meyers, 18
Attorneys' fees
  Alyeska Pipeline Service Co. v. The Wilderness Society, 91

Back pay
  Albemarle Paper Co. v. Moody, 66
Banking
  United States v. Citizens and Southern National Bank, 103
Bias in administrative adjudications
  Withrow v. Larkin, 63
Border patrol
  United States v. Brignoni-Ponce, 28
  United States v. Ortiz, 27
  United States v. Peltier, 26
Burden of proof in criminal cases
  Mullaney v. Wilbur, 32

Child support
  Stanton v. Stanton, 99

143

Church-state relations
  Meek v. Pittenger, 41
Civil rights
  Johnson v. Mississippi, 92
  Wood v. Strickland, 45
Civil Rights Act of 1964
  Albemarle Paper Co. v. Moody, 66
Civil rights damage suits
  O'Connor v. Donaldson, 53
Class actions
  Sosna v. Iowa, 55
Clayton Act
  United States v. American Building
    Maintenance Industries, 110
  United States v. Citizens and South-
    ern National Bank, 103
Closing argument
  Herring v. New York, 26
Coastal lands
  United States v. Maine, 137
Comparative negligence
  United States v. Reliable Transfer
    Co., Inc., 122
Confessions
  Brown v. Illinois, 17
Congressional investigations
  Eastland v. U.S. Servicemen's Fund,
    59
Conrail
  Regional Rail Reorganization Act
    Cases, 125
Conscientious objectors
  Serfass v. United States, 22
  United States v. Jenkins, 21
Construction industry
  Connell Construction Co., Inc. v.
    Plumbers and Steamfitters, Local
    No. 100, 106
Contempt
  Maness v. Meyers, 18
Cooperative housing stock
  United Housing Foundation, Inc. v.
    Forman, 123
Copyright Act of 1909
  Twentieth Century Music Corp. v.
    Aiken, 118
Copyright infringement
  Twentieth Century Music Corp. v.
    Aiken, 118
Corporate executives
  United States v. Park, 36
Corporate franchise taxes
  Colonial Pipeline Co. v. Traigle, 119
Corporate political campaign contribu-
  tions
  Cort v. Ash, 75

Courts-martial
  Schlesinger v. Councilman, 85
Criminal Appeals Act
  Serfass v. United States, 22
  United States v. Wilson, 20
Criminal contempt
  Muniz v. Hoffman, 114

Death penalty
  Schick v. Reed, 38
Debtor-creditor rights
  North Georgia Finishing, Inc. v. Di-
    Chem, Inc., 58
Democratic National Convention, 1972
  Cousins v. Wigoda, 71
Discharge for want of promotion
  Schlesinger v. Ballard, 98
Disclosure of evidence by the accused
  United States v. Nobles, 35
Divorce
  Sosna v. Iowa, 55
Double jeopardy
  Breed v. Jones, 23
  Serfass v. United States, 22
  United States v. Jenkins, 21
  United States v. Wilson, 20
Due process
  Goss v. Lopez, 43
  Jackson v. Metropolitan Edison Co.,
    54
  Mullaney v. Wilbur, 32
  North Georgia Finishing, Inc. v. Di-
    Chem, Inc., 58
  Weinberger v. Salfi, 134
  Weinberger v. Wiesenfeld, 97
  Withrow v. Larkin, 63
  Wood v. Strickland, 45

Economic Stabilization Act of 1970
  Fry v. United States, 121
Employment
  Albemarle Paper Co. v. Moody, 66
Enjoining state criminal proceedings
  Kugler v. Helfant, 84
Equal protection
  Stanton v. Stanton, 99
Establishment of religion
  Meek v. Pittenger, 41
Exclusionary rule
  Brown v. Illinois, 17
  United States v. Peltier, 26

Fair trial
  Murphy v. Florida, 34
Farm labor
  Saxbe v. Bustos, 136
Federal Aviation Administration
  Administrator, FAA v. Robertson, 131
Federal preemption of state antitrust laws
  Connell Construction Co., Inc. v. Plumbers and Steamfitters, Local No. 100, 106
Federal Rules of Criminal Procedure
  United States v. Nobles, 35
Federal Water Pollution Control Act
  Train v. City of New York, 137
Fifth Amendment
  Maness v. Meyers, 18
Food and drugs
  United States v. Park, 36
Food, Drug, and Cosmetic Act
  United States v. Park, 36
Foreign corporations
  Allenberg Cotton Co., Inc. v. Pittman, 120
Fourth Amendment
  Brown v. Illinois, 17
  Gerstein v. Pugh, 30
  United States v. Brignoni-Ponce, 28
  United States v. Ortiz, 27
  United States v. Peltier, 26
Free speech
  Erznoznik v. City of Jacksonville, 61
  Southeastern Promotions, Ltd. v. Conrad, 62
Freedom of association
  Cousins v. Wigoda, 71
  Eastland v. U.S. Servicemen's Fund, 59
Freedom of Information Act
  Administrator, FAA v. Robertson, 131
  NLRB v. Sears, Roebuck & Co., 128
  Renegotiation Board v. Grumman Aircraft Engineering Corp., 130
Freedom of the press
  Bigelow v. Virginia, 51
  Cantrell v. Forest City Publishing Co., 68
  Cox Broadcasting Corp. v. Cohn, 50

Government appeals in criminal cases
  Serfass v. United States, 22
  United States v. Jenkins, 21
  United States v. Wilson, 20

"Hair"
  Southeastern Promotions, Ltd. v. Conrad, 62

Immigration
  Saxbe v. Bustos, 136
  United States v. Brignoni-Ponce, 28
  United States v. Ortiz, 27
Immunity
  Wood v. Strickland, 45
Impeachment evidence
  Oregon v. Hass, 16
Impoundment
  Train v. City of New York, 137
Interrogation of suspects
  Oregon v. Hass, 16
Interstate commerce
  Allenberg Cotton Co., Inc. v. Pittman, 120
  Colonial Pipeline Co. v. Traigle, 119
  Fry v. United States, 121
Involuntary confinement of the mentally ill
  O'Connor v. Donaldson, 53
Irrebuttable presumptions
  Weinberger v. Salfi, 134

Jury instructions
  United States v. Park, 36
Jury selection
  Murphy v. Florida, 34
Jury service
  Taylor v. Louisiana, 95
Jury trial
  Muniz v. Hoffman, 114
Just compensation
  Regional Rail Reorganization Act Cases, 125
Juvenile delinquents
  Breed v. Jones, 23

Labor unions
  Connell Construction Co., Inc. v. Plumbers and Steamfitters, Local No. 100, 106
  Emporium Capwell Co. v. Western Addition Community Organization, 112
  Muniz v. Hoffman, 114
  NLRB v. J. Weingarten, Inc., 111

Legislative immunity
Eastland v. U.S. Servicemen's Fund, 59
Low- and moderate-income housing
Warth v. Seldin, 89

Medical licensing
Withrow v. Larkin, 63
Mental illness
O'Connor v. Donaldson, 53
Mergers
United States v. American Building Maintenance Industries, 110
United States v. Citizens and Southern National Bank, 103
Minimum fee schedules
Goldfarb v. Virginia State Bar, 108
*Miranda* warnings
Brown v. Illinois, 17
Oregon v. Hass, 16
Mootness
Sosna v. Iowa, 55
Movie theaters
Erznoznik v. City of Jacksonville, 61
Multimember electoral districts
Chapman v. Meier, 72
Municipal bond elections
Hill v. Stone, 74
Murder
Mullaney v. Wilbur, 32
Musical productions
Southeastern Promotions, Ltd. v. Conrad, 62
Mutual funds
United States v. National Assn. of Securities Dealers, Inc., 102

National Association of Securities Dealers
United States v. National Assn. of Securities Dealers, Inc., 102
National Labor Relations Act
Connell Construction Co., Inc. v. Plumbers and Steamfitters, Local No. 100, 106
Emporium Capwell Co. v. Western Addition Community Organization, 112
NLRB v. J. Weingarten, Inc., 111
National Labor Relations Board
NLRB v. Sears, Roebuck & Co., 128
National nominating conventions
Cousins v. Wigoda, 71

Obscenity
Erznoznik v. City of Jacksonville, 61
Hicks v. Miranda, 81
Huffman v. Pursue, Ltd., 83
One-man, one-vote
Chapman v. Meier, 72
Ownership of the seabed
United States v. Maine, 137

Pardon power
Schick v. Reed, 38
Parochial schools
Meek v. Pittenger, 41
Pay Board
Fry v. United States, 121
Penn Central Transportation Company
Regional Rail Reorganization Act Cases, 125
Preliminary hearings
Gerstein v. Pugh, 30
Presidential election, 1972
Cort v. Ash, 75
Cousins v. Wigoda, 71
Pretrial publicity
Murphy v. Florida, 34
Price fixing
Goldfarb v. Virginia State Bar, 108
Prior restraint of free speech
Southeastern Promotions, Ltd. v. Conrad, 62
Privileges and immunities clause
Austin v. New Hampshire, 65
Probable cause
Gerstein v. Pugh, 30
Public education
Goss v. Lopez, 43
Public interest groups
Alyeska Pipeline Service Co. v. The Wilderness Society, 91
Public nuisances
Huffman v. Pursue, Ltd., 83

Racial discrimination
Albemarle Paper Co. v. Moody, 66
City of Richmond v. United States, 76
Emporium Capwell Co. v. Western Addition Community Organization, 112
Railroad bankruptcies
Regional Rail Reorganization Act Cases, 125

Reapportionment
Chapman v. Meier, 72
Regional Rail Reorganization Act of 1973
Regional Rail Reorganization Act Cases, 125
Removal of state prosecutions
Johnson v. Mississippi, 92
Renegotiation Board
Renegotiation Board v. Grumman Aircraft Engineering Corp., 130
Restrictions on the franchise to taxpayers
Hill v. Stone, 74
Retroactivity
Schick v. Reed, 38
United States v. Peltier, 26
Review of three-judge court decisions
Gonzalez v. Automatic Employees Credit Union, 88
Hicks v. Miranda, 81
MTM, Inc. v. Baxley, 87
Right of privacy
Cantrell v. Forest City Publishing Co., 68
Cox Broadcasting Corp. v. Cohn, 50
Right to counsel
Faretta v. California, 25
Herring v. New York, 26
Right to hearing
North Georgia Finishing, Inc. v. Di-Chem, Inc., 58
Right to interstate travel
Sosna v. Iowa, 55
Right to jury trial
Taylor v. Louisiana, 95
Rule of divided damages
United States v. Reliable Transfer Co., Inc., 122
Rule 10b-5 of the Securities Exchange Act
Blue Chip Stamps v. Manor Drug Stores, 116

School administrators
Wood v. Strickland, 45
School expulsions
Wood v. Strickland, 45
School suspensions
Goss v. Lopez, 43
Securities
Blue Chip Stamps v. Manor Drug Stores, 116
United Housing Foundation, Inc. v. Forman, 123

Securities and Exchange Commission
United States v. National Assn. of Securities Dealers, Inc., 102
Securities Exchange Act of 1934
United Housing Foundation, Inc. v. Forman, 123
Selection of delegates to nominate presidential candidates
Cousins v. Wigoda, 71
Self-incrimination
Maness v. Meyers, 18
United States v. Nobles, 35
Self-representation
Faretta v. California, 25
Sewage treatment
Train v. City of New York, 137
Sex discrimination
Schlesinger v. Ballard, 98
Stanton v. Stanton, 99
Taylor v. Louisiana, 95
Weinberger v. Wiesenfeld, 97
Sherman Act
Goldfarb v. Virginia State Bar, 108
United States v. Citizens and Southern National Bank, 103
Social security
Weinberger v. Salfi, 134
Weinberger v. Wiesenfeld, 97
Sovereign rights of the United States
United States v. Maine, 137
Standard of criminal liability
United States v. Park, 36
Standing
Warth v. Seldin, 89
"State action" under the Fourteenth Amendment
Jackson v. Metropolitan Edison Co., 54
State aid to parochial schools
Meek v. Pittenger, 41
State employees
Fry v. United States, 121
State sovereignty
Fry v. United States, 121
State taxation
Colonial Pipeline Co. v. Traigle, 119
State taxation of nonresidents
Austin v. New Hampshire, 65
Stockholders' rights
Blue Chip Stamps v. Manor Drug Stores, 116
Cort v. Ash, 75
Student rights
Goss v. Lopez, 43
Wood v. Strickland, 45
Suburban exclusionary zoning practices
Warth v. Seldin, 89

147

Subversive activities
  Eastland v. U.S. Servicemen's Fund, 59
Summons
  United States v. Bisceglia, 32

Tax investigations
  United States v. Bisceglia, 32
Three-judge courts
  Gonzalez v. Automatic Employees Credit Union, 88
  Hicks v. Miranda, 81
  MTM, Inc. v. Baxley, 87
Title searches
  Goldfarb v. Virginia State Bar, 108
Trans-Alaskan oil pipeline
  Alyeska Pipeline Service Co. v. The Wilderness Society, 91
Tucker Act
  Regional Rail Reorganization Act Cases, 125

Unborn children
  Burns v. Alcala, 132
Unemployment compensation
  Philbrook v. Glodgett, 133
Unfair labor practices
  Emporium Capwell Co. v. Western Addition Community Organization, 112
  NLRB v. J. Weingarten, Inc., 111

Unreasonable seizures
  Gerstein v. Pugh, 30
Utility service
  Jackson v. Metropolitan Edison Co., 54

Vehicle searches
  United States v. Brignoni-Ponce, 28
  United States v. Ortiz, 27
Voting
  City of Richmond v. United States, 76
  Hill v. Stone, 74
Voting Rights Act
  City of Richmond v. United States, 76

Wage and price controls
  Fry v. United States, 121
Water pollution
  Train v. City of New York, 137
Welfare
  Burns v. Alcala, 132
  Philbrook v. Glodgett, 133
Work product doctrine
  United States v. Nobles, 35

Zoning laws
  Warth v. Seldin, 89